The
Naked
Investor

By Robert Heller

THE GREAT EXECUTIVE DREAM
THE COMMON MILLIONAIRE
THE NAKED INVESTOR

The
Naked
Investor

Cautions for Dealing with the Stock Market

Robert Heller

DELACORTE PRESS/NEW YORK

Manufactured in the United States of America

First printing

Library of Congress Cataloging in Publication Data

Heller, Robert, 1932–
    The naked investor.

        1. Investments. 2. Speculation. 3. Stock exchange.
I. Title.
HG4521.H5155   332.6'78   76-22708
ISBN 0-440-06257-8

Author's Note

This book grew originally out of my work for the *Investor's Guardian*, an excellent British publication which died an untimely death through no fault of its young, energetic and able staff—all of whom appear to have moved on to better and higher things. My attitude to matters of investment was also strongly influenced by my experience on the London *Observer* and, in particular, by my long friendship with John Davis of that newspaper. To him and to many other journalistic colleagues I owe a great debt: if I mention specifically John Thackray of New York, that is because of the unique window which he has opened on Wall Street in the past extraordinary decade. As with my earlier books, Felicity Krish has been a vital help; as with my *The Common Millionaire*, Jeanne Bernkopf of Delacorte has been as much partner as Editor, and invaluable in both capacities. The dedication, however, can only be made to the hero/victims of the events which this book primarily describes. As with those who suffered the military catastrophes of our century, the prime actors in these financial events were mostly anonymous. So I dedicate this book to

The Unknown Investor

'76-05125

Contents

Contents

FOREWORD
Once Bitten, Never Again

Failure is a better teacher than success. So the fact that the investment world failed in the seventies, for the second time in four decades, gives you as an investor a priceless opportunity. You can learn from your own mistakes and everybody else's—including mine. And you can do so in the relative comfort of an economy which isn't disfigured by endless breadlines and bankruptcies.

What you can't do is to prevent Wall Street or any other stock market from laying another egg. At the moment of writing, the professional investors, encouraged by a breath of spring in the markets, are all set to repeat the excesses of their own recent pasts. Once again, they are on the hunt for "growth stocks"— objects which don't exist now, and never did.

You—the naked investor—are under no obligation to follow the professionals back into the same jungle. The money is still there to be made, but by beating the pros, not backing them—and you can do it.

What you can do, as well, is to exert your influence as a citizen to try to prevent your government from making a mess of the world's and your country's money; or from passing new taxes and adopting other new policies that make life more difficult, and less profitable, for the willing saver.

That's what investment is: saving. If you spend less than you earn, you create capital. What you do with that capital, even leaving it under the mattress, is investment. But the mattress won't protect, and certainly won't enhance, the value of that capital. You can achieve that end through the stock market—but only by learning and using the lessons of the past.

My book isn't one of those tales told by a miracle man who made a million on the market in two years, months or days, and who seeks to make another by telling (and embroidering) the tale. To the extent that it draws on my own experience, it is the experience of another naked investor who should have known better, and often didn't—but who, with luck, will prove to have learned better.

Like everyone else, I had my successes and my failures, both at home in Britain and while living in New York, where Wall Street first started to fascinate me back in 1958. The first stock market piece I wrote for my paper in that gloomy Eisenhower season properly recorded the experts' universal despair about the market's downward career. Two days later the market staged one of the sharpest booms in its history.

That was my first lesson. The experts, it seemed, knew no more about where the market was heading than I did—and I had only just sailed in across the Atlantic.

My second lesson came from a friend who had preceded me by a few months. He constantly urged me to buy the penny stocks, dreadful things with names apparently dreamed up in Wall Street boiler rooms, that were then the rage. Of course, I didn't buy. And, of course, my friend, after a couple of hectic years, quit Wall Street with a not-so-small fortune.

That taught me never to trust the streak of yellow which naked investors like me have running down our spines. We don't back our judgment, not because it is bad, but because we are not brave. That's no way to win.

Yet in a peculiar sense I was right. The penny stocks he peddled *were* intrinsically worthless. The buying on which his fortune depended *was* a mindless response in a manipulated market. This *was* the seamy side of the boom mentality which, in the early sixties, was gathering its eventually fatal momentum.

In the late seventies, you have one paramount interest in those events. By understanding what happened then, you will be forearmed against attempts to do to you again as you were done. Better still, since the falsehoods of the failed investment ideas came from standing true principles on their heads, they can be used to illustrate exactly why those principles are true—and good.

Learning and using those principles is how the naked investor can come in out of the cold.

1 The Dividend Is the Message

For three decades, which spanned the most destructive war in history, the Western investor was haunted by another living nightmare: the fear that, just as the 1914-18 holocaust had been repeated after only twenty-one years, so the Great Crash of 1929, which wiped out his father's savings, and the Greater Depression that followed, which made further earnings and savings so hard to come by, would be replayed by history.

Thirty-five years later, in the mid-sixties, the nightmare must have seemed only that to an investor with three cars in his Westchester garage—a bad dream, far removed from the reality of ever-expanding gross national products and of a mass capitalism that generated apparently everlasting growth for the country and his own finances. He knew that a $1000 bill invested in IBM, the paradigm of the new capitalism, at its beginnings, was worth some $6.7 million in 1968; and this was no golden calf reserved for plutocrats, but a common stock held by the new masses, not only as individuals like him, but also through pension funds and mutual funds and investment trusts. Safety in numbers was the name of this new economic game, a game in which we all apparently won.

Ten years further on, in 1974, the statistics of Wall Street and, almost certainly, of our investor's portfolio, read like an inventory of Hiroshima real estate after the Bomb. By midway through the previous year, one general index of 1,500 stocks had fallen 57.2% in five years—more than *The New York Times* index had collapsed in that dreaded autumn of 1929. Even that grim statistic understated the damage. In 1968-73 the value of the dollars in which stock prices are calculated had itself declined by 26.2%. And that only measured the internal buying power of the American currency, on which worse indignities had been inflicted outside.

Between December 1968 and mid-1973, the price of gold (en route to a peak of nearly $200 in 1974) advanced from $35 an ounce to $120. This devastating devaluation of the dollar was unofficial (the U.S. Government, giving a passable imitation of King Canute, kept on pretending it hadn't happened). But the result was real enough: where, in December 1968, buying the thirty stocks listed in the Dow Jones index would have cost 28.4 ounces of gold, by July 1973 a mere 7 ounces could have picked up the same bundle.

The story was equally macabre in terms of the yen, the Swiss franc, the German mark. In July 1973 an Arab sheikh or European plutocrat owning gold could have lapped up the cream of American industry for an eighth of its 1968 cost.

What had decimated Wall Street was about to destroy savings just as surely in Frankfurt, Tokyo, Paris, Milan and London. That July, London share prices were only a fifth down from their all-time peak. Within eighteen months, the *Financial Times* index had collapsed to 146—a quarter of where it had been in 1972, a decline far more catastrophic even than Wall Street's.

The economic explanations of the disasters of 1973 and 1974 included the endless American balance of payments deficits, the consequent rise and globular swelling of the Eurodollar bubble, the consequent escalation of inflation, the consequent undermining of living standards and savings—and on, and on, until the quadrupling of oil prices sealed the catastrophe. All these global developments were crystal-clear: certainly no crystal ball was required to identify either the trends or their inevitable results.

But the stock market could have survived the massive onslaughts of economic events without staging a Second Great Crash, let alone actually outdoing the original, had it not been for the previous grotesqueries. We, the investing public, were the victims of the biggest con, the greatest confidence trick ever perpetrated, not only because the sting was in the billions, but also because so large an army of deceivers told us the tale and took a slice of the action. Stockbrokers, tipsters, bankers, hotshot salesmen, mandarins, economists, promoters, managers, journalists, politicians—the names were legion and the con so powerful that many of the insiders accomplished the ultimate coup: they conned themselves.

Just consider an ad which you may have seen midway through the awful year of 1973, published by the valiant American Stock Exchange, exhorting us customers to roll up for the greatest bunch of bargains ever seen, hundreds and hundreds of them. In rough paraphrase, it ran something like this: "You dare not refuse this offer, which we sincerely hope (for your sakes) is unrepeatable. These stocks number over 1000, and you can buy them, on the average, at a price *half* as high as you could a year ago. And that's not all! Why, these stocks haven't been so cheap since December 1966."

Amex had stood disaster on its head. The miserable facts could be seen in the price-earnings ratios (these being the number of times the earnings per share divides into the share price). At the end of April, 504 Amex stocks were selling at less than ten times earnings. The median of all the Amex offerings was only 10.39; the handful selling at the former hot ratios of 30, 40, 50, 60, 70 and more were hard to find among the masses of unloved and unwanted stocks.

But you can't keep a good salesman down. "Lower price/earnings ratios are frequently associated with greater values," the ad actually said, more in hope than conviction. Many of the bargains were "representing an exciting future. These are the younger companies which are answering the new needs of a changing society—companies offering new technologies . . ."

The insolence was staggering, especially from the viewpoint of investors who had backed "younger companies" like Viatron (the bombed-out computer terminals outfit) or Memorex (another busted flush which had once been a big deal in magnetic tape) or Litton Industries (the youthful granddaddy of all younger new technology companies, whose shares had fallen from over $100 to a feeble $10). Yet still in mid-1973 the voice of the Amex huckster was heard in the land, promising, not just growth, but growth through new technologies of which most members of Amex knew less than they did of the dark side of the moon.

4

Plainly, Amex had not even a little toe to stand on at the time when it made its sales pitch.

In the spring of 1973, in the very week the Dow Jones index broke 1000, never to see it again until 1976, an English writer, C. Gordon Tether, pinpointed the truth in a perceptive article published in the *Financial Times*. He noted that, because of the dollar's fall in value, when the 1972 index had reached the same level as the old high of 1966, "this composite collection of US stocks was in reality fetching only three-quarters of its price six years back."

Yet in 1972 the gross national product was still a fifth ahead of 1966 in real terms—so stocks had actually performed, relative to the economy, in wretched style. Tether calculated that the Dow needed to hit 1700 before U.S. investors could make up the lost ground, or lost money, of six tolerably fat economic years: that calculation goes far toward explaining why the Dow index thereafter hit a 1975 low of 632.04.

What was the value of a common stock in the years before the Second Great Crash? It couldn't lie in the dividend, since yields in all popular cases were much lower than the interest paid on savings deposits. By a curious inversion of logic, the safest and most blue chip of baskets, fit for widows, orphans and retired millionaires to place all their eggs in, often yielded among the lowest returns of all.

Nor could the value of such a stock lie in the assets, since the market capitalization of a big company generally stood well above the valuation of all its assets—fixed assets, those merely passing through and intangible ones. Conservative old Du Pont was selling at end-1972 at twice the underlying worth of the business: its factories, technology, patents, machines, unsold chemicals, inventory, net debtors, offices—the lot.

True, the replacement cost of the fixed assets is much higher than the figures in the books. But that is a point of pure academic abstraction, since nobody proposes to buy the business: only a Midas would conceivably calculate how much, say, Ford Motor's historic River Rouge plant would cost to build new, as a measure of what he will pay for it secondhand. From our angle as investors, the assets are locked in. Our concern can only be with the earnings that the assets generate.

But this merely begs another question. What price earnings? Xerox in April 1973 was selling at 50 times earnings, Polaroid at 101 times, while the common stock of McDonald's, the king of fast-food chains, was priced at 76 times earnings, a fact which bemused a writer for *Business Week*. He pointed out that "if McDonald's doubles its earnings every six years (a highly unlikely prospect), an investor who buys shares today . . . is theoretically buying earnings out to the year 2005."

Yet the hucksters advised us that the value of high-priced shares was not their present-day worth but their future price. So it was fine and dandy to pay the sun and the stars for some Wall Street bauble in the 1960s, because it would be worth the moon as well in the 1970s. Would it? A bargain deserves its name only if it costs you less than others are willing to pay now or in the reasonably near future.

That same Amex ad pointed out that 267 of the stocks listed on the exchange had paid consecutive dividends for from 10 to 125 years. This information was "for investors who focus on dividends and yields."

The Dividend Is the Message

The implication was that investors who focus on dividends and yields were some subspecies of the genus, a fuddy-duddy breed of coupon clippers who would be content with solid, stolid fare: old English sheep dogs, as opposed to greyhounds.

Which brings me to our first basic truth. You and I as investors are in duty bound to focus on dividends and yields because that, in blunt fact, is all our money buys. Yet for decades the investment community tried to divert our attention from this basic reality—for good reason. As soon as we came to care about yields again, the levels of stock prices couldn't possibly be sustained; indeed, the prices were only maintained with much difficulty even before the Second Great Crash.

The naked investor, wiser than his deceivers, had slowly cottoned on. A massive transference of share ownership took place as the stock moved from persons to institutions. The average man is much brighter than he believes when it comes to higher finance. And we investors in common stock had become progressively harder to sell even before a steep rise in interest rates dealt the *coup de grace* to a stock market founded on indefensible multiples of earnings and minute dividend yields.

The similarity between the second debacle and the first lay in the weight of money piling up on top of inflated values. The difference lay in the fact that the 1929 investors, having borrowed the money which they plunged into stocks, were consequently forced to sell, and be wiped out, by the collapse. Forty years later, investors, for the most part, had invested their own savings. These were just as effectively decimated, but the pressure to sell was far less acute, and the degree of obliteration less absolute.

7

Many of us could afford to sit among our share certificates and wait until Xerox was again able to look a dollar bill in the face. But we are unlikely to feel the same fine, careless rapture about equities ever again. Yet the quest in which we investors united still has its compulsion. We may have been sidetracked. But the simple objective remains: to be able, like our grandfathers, to save, to guard our savings and to augment those savings by placing them in other people's hands. This time, let's get it right.

2 Don't Trust Inflation When It Brings You Gifts

All investment is a would-be hedge against inflation. That is, you don't put money anywhere more sophisticated than a piggy-bank, in a wonder stock or a mere interest-bearing deposit, unless you expect to get back both your capital and a real return on the money. The special appeal of common stocks was that they allegedly guarded you against inflation far more successfully than anything else. So the investor in common stocks was presumed smarter than those who picked other, less protective forms.

Some people even stuff their all into mattresses under the illusion that cash keeps its value. Nevertheless, that is the true name of the investment game: the preservation and enhancement of cash. In the first two postwar decades you might have won the game in common stocks—although the game had far fewer winners than the investment industry claimed. But as inflation mounted to rates unseen since pre-Hitler Germany, equities proved worse than no defense. The damage was doubled, tripled and quadrupled as the

9

inflation-hedge idea proved no match for the theory of natural interest.

According to this, the "natural" rate of interest oscillates around 3% (over the centuries people have generally been prepared to accept this price for their money). Any interest above the 3% waterline contains a useful element of protection against the declining value of money. It follows that the faster money is depreciating, the higher interest rates must be—otherwise the "real" rate of interest (that's your face rate minus the rate of inflation) will fall below that natural rate of 3%.

Plainly, the speedier the fall in the value of money, the harder it is for interest rates to stay in the race. With a 20% escalation in living costs, investors should demand at least a 23% return.

But if industry pays 23%-plus on its borrowed funds, what prices must companies charge to keep profits ahead of their borrowing costs? In the reality of economic life, sky-high interest rates act as a severe curb on the profits of everybody (except bankers) and as a mighty irritant to anybody, such as a home buyer, who needs to borrow cash.

So there is an artificial barrier to the efforts of money to find its own level in terms of price. The result is that in times of rapid inflation investors as likely as not receive a *negative* return: their interest receipts are less than the amount by which inflation eats into their capital.

By the same token, borrowers are *paying* a negative rate of interest: they will actually have to repay, in real terms, less than they received—even with heavy interest charges thrown in.

You would expect, in such circumstances, a stampede to borrow, an overwhelming reluctance to lend. The true-life world doesn't behave like that. But it is true that, when interest turns negative, savers initially turn against lending: they cast about for some other home for their money, for gold coins, or goods like a new quadriphonic sound system, or debatable investments, like wolfram, or pleasing ones, like antique silver.

The common stock was promoted on the argument that earnings and dividends in industry could rise in response to economic forces, including the attacks of inflation, while fixed interest was just that—fixed at whatever rate was going at the time of investment. You might not (almost certainly would not) be able to buy equities at a dividend yield which was the equivalent of the rate of inflation plus the natural rate of interest. But the capital gains as the stock soared in value would more than offset the loss of income—and inflation plainly tended, so we were told, to make capital gains more likely.

In practice, events failed to work out so smoothly, even in the mind, let alone the market. For there is no connection between the behavior of the market and the inflation issue—or any other issue. The pattern of the stock market, like that of any market, is determined by the aggregate of a host of individual decisions, positive and negative (the decision *not* to buy a share is just as meaningful as a decision to buy). This market psychology always feeds off itself: that is, the more people who decide to sell, the greater the number of pessimists, or bears, who join the unhappy throng.

Some prevailing idea or preoccupation may infect the air at the time (like fears of inflation or hopes for peace in Southeast Asia), and that notion will affect some people. Even more certainly, it will be seized upon by those who read the entrails of the market as an explanation of the latter's behavior, *no matter what that behavior is.*

This analysis is supported by the researches of Irwin Friend and Marshall Blume of the Wharton School of Finance. Looking back over four decades, they could find no evidence of any relation between inflation and stock market levels.

There are times, true, when share prices rise as the cost of living does. But there are also times when the stock market falls while retail prices advance at a gallop. Quoted in *Business Week* in February 1975, Friend observed that "The stock market never has been an inflation hedge, and over the past eight years, it has been an utter disaster." He has an explanation, which is that high inflation increases both uncertainty and risk, which is bad for business. You could equally well argue that high interest rates (which invariably accompany high inflation) not only raise the financial overheads of business, but also, by lifting the "opportunity cost" level (that is, the worth of an alternative investment), cut the rate and number of new ventures.

There are other fundamentalist arguments. A Harvard man, John Lintner, maintains that there is good and bad inflation from the market's point of view. In good, or early, inflation, companies are able to raise prices faster than their costs. Then, since one man's price rises are another man's higher costs, profit margins come under pressure. Still worse, they enter a third stage, in which phony profits made on inventories play a bigger and bigger role in reported profits—but the companies must still pay taxes on these phantom gains.

In addition, depreciation charged on the historical

cost of plant and machinery becomes unrealistic as replacement prices soar: needs for working capital are inflated, too, even though the physical volume of turnover may not have changed. So firms get strapped for cash, and their profits suffer accordingly as the managements try to raise the funds at a time of high interest charges.

These explanations are clever and sound, and good for you to bear in mind, but somewhat beside the point. In the Great Crumple, it made no difference if profits went on rising or borrowings increased. The shares still got clobbered. Nor was this because the X-ray sensitivity of the stock market had pierced through the phony profits to the uncomfortable reality beneath.

The truth of the matter is that profits had always contained large fictitious elements, but the most transparently misleading element of all, as we saw, had been sedulously ignored on all sides. This was the fact that a million pounds or dollars of profit reported in 1973 was not the same amount, by any means, as the same sum in 1963. Nor was either million worth the same amount as the same digits reported in 1953.

Equities failed to provide a hedge against inflation, in other words, because earnings were eroded, like all other money flows or cash hoards, by the declining purchasing power of currency. Anybody who bought equities to protect the real value of his capital must have presumed that the value of the earnings or the assets he was *currently* buying would be at least maintained in real terms. But the boards of directors dutifully reported the shining achievements of every year in the unreal terms of depreciating money.

To take a case in point, no stock had a more devoted following of inflation-hedgers than International

Business Machines—and few managements hedged more effectively. From 1968 to 1973, profits after tax ostensibly rose by 81%, and earnings per share by three-quarters. But in that period United States prices were escalating by 4.8% annually. The dollar of 1973 was worth 78.2 cents in the money of 1968.

In those five years, IBM earnings had grown by only half as much as appeared in the books—which means that the compound rate of growth had fallen by *more* than half to a rather ordinary figure of around 6½% annually.

IBM was a High Altar of the cult, far ahead of the typical shrine. Most other examples had no real growth in earnings worth discussing. If we invested in a company which exactly kept pace with inflation (with stock prices exactly reflecting the movement of assets and earnings), we would have got back exactly what had been put in: no more, no less. Our return would thus have been confined to our dividends—which for supposed growth stocks were very much lower than the yields available on fixed interest.

Even that might have been tolerable, assuming that the loss in yields was less than the erosion in the capital value of the fixed interest investment. On the one hand, say, you put $100 into a bond and get back the post-inflation equivalent of $80 plus $10 of interest. That $90 is a much worse deal than placing $100 in equities and getting back $100 plus $5 of dividends (and that's without taking differential rates of tax as between dividends and capital gains into account).

But all too many stocks recorded *negative* growth —that is, their earnings failed to rise by as much as retail prices, either over the whole of postwar time, or over selected periods (and it is only the selected period between the purchase and sale of a share that interests the investor).

The earnings of the Ford Motor Company were no higher in 1968, in inflated money terms, than in 1956. The increase in their money value, again, was negligible in 1971. Even after a strong surge, the Ford profits in 1973 were only 30% higher than eight years before—hardly the kind of behavior to which Henry Ford I was accustomed.

The reality of profits becomes even dimmer if allowance is made for the various gimmicks, devices and deceits that corporate leaders adopted to make their inflation-boosted profits seem higher still. Cynics have not missed the significance of industry's upsurge of interest in "inflation accounting," which seeks to *reduce* reported profits by removing inflationary elements, at precisely the time the stock market ceased to care about earnings per share.

When earnings no longer counted in market terms, managements grew more interested in money inside, as opposed to outside, the business. They promptly turned to ways of reducing their taxation.

The most remarkable illustration of this belated conversion was the big 1973 switch from FIFO (first in, first out) to LIFO (last in, first out). If a company sold $100 of product for which it used materials which were valued in its inventory at either $25 (on old stuff) or $50 (the new), under FIFO it took the earlier and cheaper price in calculating costs and profits; with LIFO, the later and dearer price. In 1955 only one American major company in three valued its inventory on a last-in-first-out basis. By 1972 the proportion was lower still: only a quarter of the majors used this method, which has the effect, in inflationary times, of reducing profits.

As the cash squeeze tightened in 1973, companies like Du Pont and the Firestone tire firm spotted the error of their long-established ways. By moving over to LIFO, Du Pont (which enjoyed a reputation for conservative accounting beforehand) slashed its first-half earnings per share by a mighty 19%. The gains in cash flow, because taxes fell along with profits, were also mighty: Firestone, for instance, improved its flow by a projected $46 million in 1974.

Now did these giants of American capitalism previously stick with FIFO because they were unfortunately ignorant of LIFO's advantages? Or were they less interested in cash flow than in showing high earnings, on which the value of their shares and their executives' stock options could be based? The least cynical of us can pick the right answer.

Depreciation itself, just like the switch to LIFO, is nothing more than a method of avoiding tax. Nobody pretends that the depreciation money is actually set aside in a little tin box exclusively for the replacement of beat-up machinery. Nobody pretends, either, that the standard formulas for depreciation bear any relation to the actual life of individual machines.

It's just an accepted convention designed to allow enough untaxed money to pile up for the replenishment of capital. If the depreciation percentage were charged on replacement costs—as industrialists and accountants began to urge—the untaxed funds would be much greater. By the same token, any scheme that asserts that inventories, though they have doubled, tripled or quadrupled in value since purchase, have actually not augmented the company's wealth at all (as accountants agreed, too) is taking the fictions of accountancy into the realms of dreamland. And bad dreamland is where naked inflation-hedgers, contemplating the inflationary evaporation of profits, along with the inflationary disappearance of earnings, must have thought themselves to be. A 19% fall in earnings like Du Pont's is not, after all, much of a hedge against inflation, or anything else.

So again, the lesson is that inflation in itself never had any connection with the case for equities. It was merely one of the sales pitches—it turned out to be the most disastrous—and it is an argument which you may safely ignore in your future investment policy. Whatever you won on the inflationary swings, and that was less than it seemed, was wiped out on the inflationary roundabouts—and it always will be.

3 When the Yield Breaks, the Value Will Fall

Among the many services of *Fortune* magazine to American business has been its annual roll of honor. This is the 500, a list of the magnificent and the mighty in United States industry, ranked by sales, ranging (in 1974) from General Motors of Detroit, with $35,798,289,000 of sales, to Avery Products of San Marino, California, with $242,711,000.

A few years ago, *Fortune* added a column which undid much of its previous benefaction. It was called "total return to investors." It assessed company growth by the gross return before tax to an investor, measured by the capital gains and dividends received over the period. Even in euphoric days on the stock market, many big companies reward their shareholders with rates of return that don't justify the risks of equity investment. In off years for stocks, most equity investors have only pitiful yields. But the *Fortune* reckoning was worse than pitiful in 1974: it was disastrous.

Among the top fifty of the elite, ten members in good standing had produced a negative return over the period from 1963. Their dividends had failed to compensate for the drop in their share prices compared to ten years before. And this, remember, was in money terms, not in the more realistic language of post-inflation currency.

Another eleven of the inner circle couldn't make the grade of a 3½% annual growth, just enough to double the investor's money after twenty years. Only a dozen members of the Hall of Sales Fame had achieved double-digit results for the stockholders since 1963. They were led by Atlantic Richfield, an oil company which had shot out of nowhere to achieve a 17.52% return. The venerable Eastman Kodak, the company largely ignored while all eyes were on Polaroid, came in second with 17.13% per annum.

Even a double-digit yield takes at least seven years to double a man's money. So four-fifths of the greatest of the great had failed an elementary test of investment. The crowned head of the industrial kingdom, General Motors, had returned to its stockholders, before tax and in depreciating currency, an annual figure of 0.3% over the decade. At that rate, an investor of 1963 in Detroit's finest would have been forced to wait until the year 2222 to double his dollars: and what will your dollar be worth then?

There is more to the Motors statistics than meets the eye. Take any year in the seventies, and a decade's return from an investment in GM, while quite respectable, was never anything to drag investors away from savings bonds in a hurry. Was there some underlying force whose movements explain 1974's Infinitesimal Total Return?

The answer can be approached through a parable. Imagine that you had advanced a friend some cash to develop his business: the manufacture and marketing of electronic crystal balls. He can't pay much in interest right now, because the room for expansion in the shed at the bottom of his garden is limited. But he holds out the prospect of a gratifying rise with each upward step.

As he advances first to his garage, then to a loft down the road, finally to an old rubber pants factory, and so on ever upwards, you will receive more and more—until eventually the yield on your original parcel of cash will top the highest interest rate on earth.

Not a bad bargain, you might think, reclining in your garden chair and hearing the comforting noises of busy labor from the next-door garage. There is, of course, a snake in your Eden. The dividends, as they rise, will attract more attention from the officials appointed by the State to deprive the well-meaning citizen of a goodly percentage of his income.

But your crystal-gazing friend has thought of that, too. His deal offers the prospect of capital gains, taxable at a lower rate. He promises to repay the money at the same dividend yield at which you started. From that oath, you can derive some alluring arithmetic. The starting yield was 2%. If the friend's projections prove correct, the profits will increase by 20% annually. This means that in about three and a half years your yield could be 4%, and the price of buying you out will be double the original loan.

Another forty-two months takes you to the seven-year payoff. The yield will be 8%, and the value four times that of the initial investment. Despite the doublings, the yield will still be far from dramatic; for 8% return before tax is strictly humdrum. But it's obviously worth putting up with meager interest, especially *taxable* meager interest, because of the delight of the multiplier effect, every percentage point of extra interest being instantly translated into a 50% rise in capital value.

All goes well in this parable up to a point. The profits rise by the promised 20% with a regularity which speaks well of the crystal balls. But in the small print you discover that your friend, while bound to raise the dividend, is under no obligation to match its growth to the profits.

He doesn't want to lose your goodwill; he might need some more of your money one day. So he keeps the dividend rising quite briskly—only, year after year it falls behind the growth in profits, until the compound rate of increase comes, not to 20%, but 7%.

You now face the unpleasant conclusion that instead of quadrupling your money in seven years, you will only double it in a decade. What seemed a marvelous investment is no more than a dull drag—and you make one eternal vow: never again to place any of your hard-earned savings in such deceitful ventures.

A fanciful tale, you may think, but it is stark reality. The whole account is an abstraction from real life, a rendering that explains why the median return to investors on *Fortune*'s 500 fell from 10.12% for the 1962-72 decade to almost half—5.22%—for the ten years 1963-73. The story can be picked up from a list I saw in the summer of 1973 of "consistent growth stocks out of favor."

There were seventeen of these pearls. Their most marked "consistency" was that growth in dividends had lagged far behind the rises in earnings per share. The minimum figure qualifying these stocks for "consistent growth" was 12.2% annually. Of the seventeen, only three had achieved this rate of progress in dividends. In all cases, however, the stocks had been bought on infinitesimal yields, presumably because buyers thought the future increase in profits would be faithfully multiplied into capital gain.

But the multiplier may not be a constant, even though it was in our parable. The borrower in that story agreed to buy back the security on the same basis of valuation. The market makes no such promise. You may always find a lower multiplier than you paid being applied. It will be applied, what's more, to a lower dividend than you would have received if the profit growth had been placed where your dividend check comes out.

This dual risk must exist even when interest rates are relatively stable. But when interest rates embark on wider, faster and larger swings, like an Olympic hammer thrower limbering up, the risks become financially suicidal. The upward oscillations of interest rates in the early seventies, as governments sought to kill the inflationary dragon they had created, turned the built-in equity drag into a free fall without a parachute.

When interest rates head for the skies, equity markets are bound to be depressed, partly because higher interest rates spell tight money, and tight money means less loose cash lying around to invest in stock markets; partly because the two conditions (usury and tightness) usually spell an economic crisis, which discourages investors; partly because high interest charges make profits and dividends harder to earn (especially at a time of economic crisis); partly because a stock that looks worth buying on a 2½% yield when fixed interest rates are 5% looks much less attractive when the 5% doubles.

Would you accept a yield of less than 5% on an equity when a fixed return of 10% is waiting in the wings? But that rise from 2½% to 5% in the acceptable yield of the common stock means it will *halve* in value. It follows that the higher yielding the equity, the less vulnerable it is to sharp upward movements in the price of money. And this truth, alas, has unsavory consequences for the low-yielding growth stock.

The low yielder is likely to be badly affected on two counts. First, the concept or cult of growth suffers a cyclical knock as various shooting stars of the past plunge into the sea. Second, shares offering minimal yields must fare worse than those whose dividends are worth taking home to the bank, because of the impact of the forces in our parable.

To take those "consistent growth stocks out of favor" again, their norm for dividend growth had been around 7% over the years. That rate of expansion still leaves a 1.5% or 2% dividend looking skinny (at 3% or 4%) after ten years of successful corporate enterprise. The never-in-favor, inconsistent, no-growth stock with a 10% yield will also sink somewhat when interest rates surge to double figures. But it won't collapse to the same extent as the onetime people's pet.

The wayward behavior of interest rates was no accident which befell mankind in the mid-sixties. Basic causes were present that we might have spotted, or that at least should have been pointed out to us by the expert few. But the tendency of the experts during the Big Bubble was the same as that of the amateurs: to recognize that stock markets bore some relation to the movement of national and world economies, but to assume that the relationship was like that of barometers and the weather.

That is, when business was good, the market (usually getting to the starting line before the economy) boomed ahead; when business turned bad, the market usually led and pointed the way downward. The financial relationship between different investments whose common denominator was a rate of return received strangely less attention. Stock market philosophers would prate about coming rallies, oblivious to the rise in interest rates. Or solons would cluck their tongues about the market's irreversible depression, when declining interest rates made recovery certain.

In early 1975 interest rates around the world, led by the United States, were falling. This single, signal fact placed a floor under the depressed markets in London and New York. As soon as a market rise became credible, it became anticipated—hence the astonishing blast-off in prices on both sides of the Atlantic. These events were all the more predictable, although very few people predicted them, because the mechanism of money, apparently mysterious, actually works quite clearly.

The price of money is the rate of interest. As with any other commodity, the price (or interest rate) tends to rise when the demand exceeds the supply, and fall when the supply exceeds the demand. The twist with this particular commodity lies with governments. They can fix the current price of money in a fairly arbitrary manner (because they control the central banks), and they can also control the supply of money, by rationing or expanding it in many crude and sophisticated ways.

One crude method of expansion is to spend more

than they take from the taxpayer. Unless the government can borrow genuine savings to fill the gap, it has to print money in various forms. You would expect such a sharp increase in supply to result in a fall in price. But a drop in interest rates in reasonable economic times will stimulate higher demand for money. And unless the system continues to feed this demand with more and more money, interest rates will start rising again under the pressure of demand from the private sector and government.

All through the sixties the United States fed the world with money. Other countries, notably Great Britain, did more than their bit to help. But Americans, by persistently overspending at home on public account, and by matching this domestic overspend abroad, were the main contributors to a global profligacy which saw the Free World money supply *double* in three years.

Since world output did nothing of the sort, massive inflation followed. This placed double pressure behind interest rates. The initial push came from government. As the central bankers of the Federal Reserve, faced with large Federal budget deficits, tried to curb the total growth of the money supply, they squeezed the amounts available to other borrowers, mainly corporations. This placed the latter in a painful predicament. The squeeze hit them at a time when inflation was increasing their demand for funds. So interest rates went on rising—and the higher the rate of inflation, the more investors tried to avoid being fobbed off with negative interest rates.

The supply of funds from private sources, in these conditions, will initially either dry up, or wash around in great tides in search of the best rates going, if those private sources cannot obtain a greater yield than the rate of inflation. The efforts of governments to mop up surplus money drove up its price at exactly the same time as investors, consciously or unconsciously, were yearning for positive returns.

The consequences for common stocks were inevitable. As the supply of money was squeezed, and its price was forced up, the nourishment for the last stages of the equity boom disappeared. Where was the stopping place for stocks, whose yields had long since ceased to bear any rational relationship to other investments? Would the Dow drop to 600, or 500, or 400, or (as some of the professional pessimists argued) 300? Suddenly, the dividends began to appear as the only safety nets in sight.

For two decades, the conventional wisdom had held that, because of high taxation, especially on investment income, the dividend was irrelevant. Just as property investors were drawn by the magnet of promised capital gains, so stockholders were taught that income was no asset—rather, high dividends were a positive liability. Growth company management was based on the nice thesis that stockholders who hate taxable dividends would far rather have green-fingered directors investing the profits, free of income tax, to make all their gardens grow.

The drawback, the catch-22 of the investment world, is this: if share ratings relate more to dividend growth than to expansion of earnings, a policy of plowing back profits (instead of paying them out as dividends) will ultimately defeat the plow-back policy's own objective—which is presumably to raise the share price.

Even in an era when people allegedly shunned dividends like mononucleosis, many investors went on holding and buying their blue chips for those supposedly unregarded payments. Even that is not the crucial point. For those who genuinely did shun the income, the dividend yield, whether they knew it or not, was a decisive factor in establishing value. At the end of the day, and at the beginning for that matter, you will only accept low yields because you believe, in the first place, that the crop of dividends will grow, and, in the second place, that the market will apply the same basis of valuation as today's (if not a higher one) to that crop.

If (on the first count) the yield does not rapidly rise, and consequently you are proved wrong on the second count, too, any wise child can tell you what you get. You get investors as unhappy as the hero in the parable when his surefire investment proved to have a built-in drag. To put it another way, you get "consistent growth stocks out of favor," that's what.

4 A Fool and His Money
Are Closely Identified

Investors have always been interested in growth.
They view investment as a horticultural process: the
money is planted in the earth and bears fruit in due
season. Growth in the true farmer's sense of making
two blades of corn sprout where one grew before is
easy enough to understand. But growth in the stock
market is a more complicated matter.

For a start, is it growth of the company or of your
own money that you want? It might seem that the two
invariably go hand in hand. But there are several and
savage exceptions to this rule. And even if great
corporate growth did unfailingly produce territorial advances in the company's stock, a big question would go
begging: what does great growth, or any growth at all,
mean for the corporation? Growth by acquisition is
growth of a kind, without doubt. But is the farmer
who makes two ears of corn sprout instead of one truly
worth no more than the man who doubles up purely
by buying the farm next door?

Dynamism in a company can exist in several different dimensions, not necessarily all at the same time. Assets can pile up; sales can multiply; profits can soar in gross total; or, divided by the number of shares in issue, profits can rise in terms of earnings per share; the number of employees can be enlarged; the return on capital or on sales can be pushed, pulled or kicked upward.

All or any of these figures can be presented to you as a prize achievement, a mark of corporate splendor and progress. Yet plainly the "goodness" of a 200% growth rate on any of these dimensions can vary according to cases—vary so much that what's good in Case One is downright disgraceful in Case Two.

Which of the following two companies, for instance, deserves the growth prize? Company A, with no acquisitions of much weight, increases its sales in four years by a quarter, its capital employed by 11% but its profits by a remarkable 371%. Company B, on the other hand, boosts its sales by 412%, its capital by 385% and its profits by 255%: so both profit margins and return on capital decline. Any holding company chairman, any controlling investor, any common man or woman with a mite in the business, must surely value Company A's growth performance and its management far above Company B—or would they?

The mysterious A and B were one and the same firm, both before and into an acquisitive phase. The stock market, it turned out, made the appropriate judgment on A and B. In the summer of 1972, the stock lay lower than in 1968, before the big buys began.

A modest $1000 inheritance deposited in the stock at the peak in 1964 would have been worth $3702 four years later. Left alone, the nest egg would then have dwindled mildly in cash terms and quite severely in purchasing power. In contrast, anybody who had arrived on the company's ground floor saw $1000 climb to $16,000 in a few enchanting years as the group was hauled from near bankruptcy into riches.

That sixteen-times capital gain is one real and wholly delightful form of growth—but it's not a direct measure of management. That is the nub. There are two kinds of expansion: shareholders' growth, shown by our example in its Company A phase, and managers' growth, as in the Company B period.

Type A growth is characterized by supercharged *increase in the returns from available assets*, Type B growth by *expansion in the assets themselves*. Real growth in management is concerned with the relationship between these two types: how to use the new resources created by organic growth to purchase new assets (through amalgamation or otherwise); how far to finance Type B growth by raising more money, through borrowings or issues of new shares (as happens in most take-overs); the optimum balance between the two types of growth; how much Type B expansion can be done without weakening, by diluting management effort and the earnings themselves, the essential Type A base.

In all those areas wrong decisions can easily be made, from which wrong deeds automatically follow; whereupon the stock market collectively refuses to turn thumbs up, or turns them decisively down.

It follows that you and I, as investors, are wildly uninterested in managers' growth for its own sake. All the effort expended by stock market experts upon fundamental analysis, replete with five-year forecasts of everything from cash flow and capital expenditure to earnings per share and dividend payout, is largely beside our point. All these figures, anyway, will be calculated in depreciating currencies, unless world economic affairs improve out of all recognition. Thus the birds in the bush will be worth considerably less in terms of purchasing power than the one in the hand, even if the management promises come true.

You should be interested in only one corporate statistic: the real, noninflationary increase in the value of your piece of paper between the moment of purchase and the hour when you either value the holding or the selling of it. At least that's the theory of the investor's true interest. The practice is more than somewhat different, because most of us have the unhelpful habit of forgetting or ignoring what we *really* paid, or what we could *actually* receive for the stock. Experience shows, too, that most stockholders are often totally indifferent to the misuse of their money by bumbling and fumbling men.

The shock suffered by investors in Consolidated Edison, when that rock of ages failed to pay a dividend, was all the greater because they had missed the mounting evidence of misconduct in the great utility's affairs. Nothing short of cataclysm will shake the faith of the investor committed to a national institution. Those who held Du Pont stock, and had seen no increase in their quarterly dividend from 1966, when it touched an annual figure of $6.00, to 1974, when it was still only $5.50, almost certainly never ceased for a single minute to feel deep loyalty and gratitude to the board of directors.

Reality is often a painful subject, and since investment (or the disposal of money) is especially sensitive, its practitioners are addicted to flights from uncomfortable truths. In one imbroglio of the tangled seventies, a writer thus declared trenchantly that one thing that must "have impressed itself on shareholders' minds is the share price . . . those who were in during the early years did wonderfully well, but the price has never reached more than half its 1969 peak." The aforesaid shareholders promptly proved him wrong by flocking to the side of the management under question.

It's doubtful whether many individual shareholders had *anything* "impressed on their minds" by the behavior of the share price. Most probably felt (1) that the company's growth had continued to serve them well, despite the post-1969 calamities; and (2) that, even if the wonders *had* ceased since then, the future miracles would be equally electrifying, thanks to the management genius which had served them so wonderfully in the past.

The reason for illogical attachments to antigrowth investments is self-evident. Any other stance would have forced the above holders to recognize that, if they owned the shares before 1969, they should have sold them in that year; while, if they bought later, at any price above the dismal levels plumbed during the imbroglio, they shouldn't have done so. If you are stuck in a "growth" investment which has grown in reverse, you are asked to confess that you've been a fool—and, much worse, a fool with your money.

If you can accept that pain, your hurt will the more rapidly disappear—it's just like having the dentist remove an infected tooth, except that you don't need an anesthetic. There's only one question to ask if you own a stock or a mutual fund, originally bought at $100 and now standing at $50 (or any other mortifying price). That question is, would I be willing to buy that investment today at that figure? If the answer is No—and it will nearly always be a resounding one—sell the investment, keep the record of the loss for the tax man and use the money for another investment, a new hi-fi or a meal at Lutece: anything, other than let it decay simply to protect your psyche.

But money evokes deep and potent psychological associations, which for all anyone knows may stem back to early memories of being breast-fed or not breast-fed. The subject easily provokes an emotionally derived confusion in otherwise well-balanced and incisively intelligent minds. Sensibility rather than sense rules in these matters; it affronts our sensibility to admit to a mistake about money.

The big talk about growth is only a euphemism about money, anyway. The growth deception works in several ways. It explains, for example, the paradox of the inflated portfolio, which is common during any period of riotous stock rises, such as the more globular years of the Big Bubble. In those swollen days, almost any of us asked about our results could trot out a gorgeous litany of capital gains. Added together, however, the golden gains usually toted up to something more modest than the string of triumphs led either listener or speaker to believe. Our memory blanks out our failures and records only our triumphs.

Investment triumphs for the growth-minded investor, in any case, often have nothing to do with the pursuit of growth in the corporate sense, but merely with chance bonanzas, sometimes even of a *nongrowth* variety.

This puzzle can be clarified by the case of a private investor who works in a university department of economics. Let's call him Mr. Pareto, after the never-to-be-forgotten Italian economist who discovered the law of the significant few and the irrelevant many (roughly, that 20% of everything we do yields 80% of all the benefits we get). Our Mr. Pareto reckoned he was "in a better position than the average investor to interpret economic information." He had achieved a 50% capital gain in not much more than five months—at a time when 5% would have been exceptional.

What did his portfolio hold? There were three deadbeat investments which had brought home no bacon at all. One fair gainer was up 22.4%. A parcel of gold shares had risen by 65%. And a single industrial purchase had soared by 237%. On the face of it, Mr. Pareto had shown excellent economic judgment at least once—gold stocks were among the outstanding investments of this epoch.

But gold mines do not square with orthodox growth theory. They might or might not report higher earnings: it didn't matter. The shares responded not to the corporate performance, but to prospects for a rise in the gold price.

You bought these equities if you thought (very sensibly) that the finance ministers and central bankers of the West would so bungle their jobs as to cause a flight from depreciating paper currency into solid yellow metal. For those who (like American citizens at the material time) couldn't own gold itself legally, mining shares were the next best thing. But this indirect route into gold was the only attraction of the companies, which lacked any of the usual characteristics of the cultist equity: no marketing, no hotshot management, no dynamic strategies—just holes in the right parts of the earth.

Still, all credit to our economist investor, Mr. Pareto, for spotting that the undervaluation of gold was sure to lead to an upward valuation of gold shares. But setting aside the gold, let's examine the Pareto jewel: the industrial share that gained 3.4 times. This was a once-noted furniture manufacturer which, by epic mismanagement, had almost totally denuded itself of earnings. A brand-new management team arrived on the scene, breathing fire, slaughter and noble resolutions. Within a couple of years, the stock (the newcomers held healthy options) more than doubled. Flushed with success, the new men proceeded to lose the best part of a cool million in two years, and the shares slid down to just above vanishing point. (The new management team did vanish.) From this abysmal level, the shares staged the spectacular recovery from which Mr. Pareto benefited.

Among any group of shares that have sunk to a few cents, a few will rebound phenomenally. But there's a snag: for every sparrow that becomes an eagle, several others become sparrow pie—and all the learning of all the books in all the libraries of all the economists can't tell which sparrow will be which.

Just like gold shares, "recovery" stocks don't fit the general profile of corporate or economic growth. But then, most growth companies don't fit the profile, either. Every standard measure of managers' growth has one disadvantage or another from our investing angle. Expansion in sales probably won't be any use unless net income rises, too. The same goes, in spades, for any increase in assets or capital employed.

The advance in net income, in turn, is of little use, so any analyst would argue, unless earnings per share grow as well. An increase of the latter, moreover, benefits nobody unless turned into a rise in the share price. A rise in the stock, to complete the round, is no good to man or beast unless it lasts long enough for you to take your profit.

Finally, all these measures except the last can be fiddled with. Rises in net income or in earnings per share are in the lap, not of the gods, but of the directors and their friendly auditors. That being so, the nature of real, true or genuine growth is shrouded in fog.

At the beginning of the seventies, when the Great Crumple was only a growing cloud on the horizon, my own magazine, *Management Today*, tried to clear away these mists. We looked at the biggest companies to discern which had shown authentic growth, as opposed to doing it with mirrors. We showed up many of the pitfalls of any effort to bring scientific objectivity to bear.

For a start, if you compare companies over any long period (1960-69 was taken), you give an unfair advantage to firms that had a rotten time the first year and prospered the last. The other way around—where the first year was great and the last horrible—the company will suffer badly in any comparisons.

In practice, there aren't too many of these injustices. In most cases, firms were fairly treated when tested by our definition of real growth. We insisted that the company should have boosted its pretax profits by 176% over the period—doubling in real terms, after allowing for inflation. The return on shareholders' equity (net income as a percentage of the capital which belonged to the investors) had to be at least maintained from first to last. Growth had to be reasonably consistent: profits were only allowed to fall or stagnate for two years out of the nine.

By no stretch of the imagination was this a demanding test. But two-thirds of the companies failed to double their profits in real terms, and 14% weren't even earning as much in 1969 as nine years before. Only sixteen firms, a 28% handful, passed the tests of consistency and profitability as well.

Applying similar criteria produces similar results in any capitalist economy. In *unreal* terms, there is abundant growth. In the *real* terms of constant money and continuous expansion, good growers are few and depressingly far between. Which points to an inescapable conclusion.

We investors in the sixties and early seventies were little wiser than the Lewis Carroll crew who took part in the hunting of the snark. We were all misled by the temper of the times. But we didn't know what we were looking for, we were led by people who knew just as little, and we were likely to be sidetracked by irrelevancies. Like the snark-hunters, we followed the ringing of the Bellman's bell: it tolled for us.

The real growth, in shareholders' terms, didn't lie in intelligent investment in properly identified corporate situations but in successful speculation. Mr. Pareto, with his red-hot recovery stock and his gold stocks, was in with a better chance, not because of his greater economic skills, but because he cared only for private monetary growth. This places him in sharp and profitable contrast to nonspeculators who look for a steady, strongly upward growth trend in a company—but don't identify the growth they seek, and in any event won't gain any personal advantage from the find.

Even where there is real growth, it does not follow, as we have seen and will see again, that the share price will reflect that reality. Where the growth is unreal, reality will catch up in the only place it can, and the place that hurts you most: the price of the stock.

Surely, you must be thinking, there are exceptions

to the rule—genuine, everlasting, real growth stocks? Well, one of the most successful investors I know, whose own company's stock used to sell at a price-earnings ratio of well over 40, was once confronted (by me) with the proposition that no stock is ever worth a 40 multiple. To this he retorted, impeccably, that none was worth 30. And the story of the Xerox Corporation, a prime long-term growth case if ever there was one, bears him out.

A book published in February 1975 under the encouraging title *You Can Still Make Millions in the Stock Market* extolled the fortune which the writer, Samuel Mitchell, had made from a modest investment in Xerox. If you got in on the ground floor (as Mitchell did), fantastic! Starting with a purchase of 100 Haloid (the predecessor of Xerox) for $30 a throw, Mitchell worked his way to $4 million in under two decades—or rather, Xerox worked his way.

Several times along the route, Mitchell checked with the management to ensure that he was still on course. Each time he was satisfied, intellectually and financially. But the postpublication story does not have a happy ending: the whole Mitchell thesis—that Xerox, "like Ol' Man River . . . keeps rolling along at a growth rate unprecedented for a multi-billion dollar corporation"—was tested and found wanting. When Xerox acquired the Californian computer firm, Scientific Data Systems, Mitchell "casually said to Peter [McColough, the Xerox boss] some time later, 'We paid a helluva price for SDS' and he [McColough] added quite casually, 'We needed it Sam.'"

They needed it like a hole in the head. In 1975 the $900 million computer buy was erased from Xerox's future in one of the costliest write-offs and acquisition failures in corporate history. To *Forbes* magazine, quoted approvingly by Mitchell, McColough had said, "It was absolutely essential for Xerox to have a computer capability to reach the objectives we have set for the seventies." Unless the brave decision to ax the computer division had been taken, Xerox wouldn't have been able to meet any objectives in the seventies, or the eighties for that matter. As it was, the total return to investors in the 1964-74 decade was a feeble 5.34% annually. Mitchell's money wouldn't even have doubled over the period; Procter & Gamble, a giant long before Haloid's early, unnoticed growth began, did better by investors.

Unlike Mitchell and other residents on the 1964 ground floor, any later Xerox buyer at the peak of any one year had to wait until 1972 to double his money. At any point after 1964, you could not buy this wonder stock *regardless of price*, secure in the knowledge that it would fetch handsomely more at any time that you wished to sell in the next five years. The worst error was to buy the stock when it was most gushingly advocated—when it was selling at its proudest price-earnings multiples. From 1964-69, the multiple rose as high as 71, and never fell below 33. In the next five years, the multiple never got above 54, and slipped as low as 27 (in 1970) before the 12 times calamity of 1974.

That explains the two linked mysteries—the disappointment of many investors who jumped aboard Xerox in the 1960s, and the failure of the share price to keep in step with the corporation's bounding growth. As the years went on, investors simply grew less and less willing to give Xerox the highest accolades of "prime long-term growth." They were not merely bored.

The figures for earnings per share show that some anchor was tugging at the company.

In the three years 1964-66, earnings per share jumped by 89%. In the four years to 1969, growth was down to 66%. In the next four years, to 1972, the figure slipped again, to 52%. Finally, the three years 1972-74 saw a 32% advance. Behind the statistics lay the inevitability of arithmetic. An extra $281.55 million of sales doubled the company from its 1964 base. The same increment in 1973, when competition had expanded (though not too formidably), and markets were more saturated, added less than 10% to the volume. And $280 million of new business, because of the saturation, was no easier to win than when the same sales gain doubled the company. The lesser growth prospects in its own market were presumably among the prime forces pushing Xerox fatefully into computers.

This company, no worse and mostly much better than other sizable corporations, demonstrates the difficulty of living up to a growth stock's own growth record. The intoxicating price-earnings ratios it once commanded only made sense if the company could not only maintain, but also accelerate its growth.

The final break usually comes when some unexpected upset, of the kind that comes to all companies and men, acts as a trigger, if not the Scientific Data Systems fiasco, then a low punch from the antitrust authorities. The case of Xerox, however, may not convince the pure growth enthusiast. After all, its performance *did* decline in relative terms over the years. What if it had been an exception to the law of diminishing returns from increasing size; what if it hadn't been burdened by comparison with its own supercharged early years? Wouldn't Xerox then have justified, if not its multiples of 70, at least the average rating of 40 or so?

Alas, the evidence won't support this comforting theory, either. I know an outstanding example of a company whose real performance improved over the years, but whose market behavior was as disappointing, and as disillusioning to growth theorists, as that of Xerox.

My antihero is the Beecham Group—purveyor of Brylcreem and Macleans toothpaste to the American market—which in the fiscal year 1964-65 was already a star company. That year the stock, too, was well-regarded—but only reasonably so. In July 1965 the dividend yield was 5%, a high figure by the standards of the equity cult in full flower. By July 1968, the dividend yield was down to a Lilliputian 1.84%, and the earnings multiple, only 18 three years before, was a relatively dizzy 30.

Would you have said that Beecham was a bad buy at 30 times earnings? From the fiscal year then just completed until 1972, the earnings per share rose by 17% a year. People who pounded into Beecham at a multiple of 30 times earnings in 1968, if they had known they were buying a dead-sure 17% earnings growth, would never have considered pounding right out again. Damned good show, they'd have said. And they would have been absolutely wrong.

To see why, backtrack to 1964-65. From that point to 1971-72, Beecham was a model of goodness and consistency. Profits before tax more than tripled; earnings per share also tripled; true, the percentage return on capital declined from 45 via a 49.7 peak to 40.8—but that was still marvelous by most industrial standards, British or American.

The lowest annual increase in earnings per share was 11% in the third year of the series. The highest was 23% in the sixth year—the one before last. Performance tended to get better with time, mainly because of the profits that poured in from a phenomenally rich family of synthetic penicillins.

In the four years from the 1965 fiscal year, earnings per share rose by 73%; in four years from 1968, the increase was 89%. But (which is the peculiar and critical point) the share price moved completely differently.

From 1964 the stock's four-year-high-to-high performance was a 207% gain: from 1969 to 1972 the score was only 41%. It can't be argued that investors sensed that miracle drug wonders were coming, and jumped off the gravy train as soon as the good news came through into the profits. The strange behavior of the share price hinged entirely on the status of the shares—which is where the story began, with Beecham selling at a multiple of 30 in July 1969.

Suppose that Beecham had never sold above, or below, a multiple of 18 over the entire seven years. The share price would still have tripled over the period (remember, the earnings did), but it would have taken far longer for the peaks to be reached. For instance, the 1968 high would have been delayed until 1971. So money placed on the Beecham bet up to 1968 anticipated something like three years of further exceptional growth.

Whether the bet was wise depended on whether, three years on, investors would *still* think it worth their while to discount three whole years of future advance. They didn't. The nearest the multiple ever came to 30 in any subsequent July (the month Beecham files its annual reports) was in 1971, when it hit 25. Even at its July 1965 multiple of 18, this share had been well ahead of the market. But for most of the later years of shining and accelerating business success, the stock was anything up to twice as expensive as the average counter.

That explains its falling rate of capital gain and rising rate of investor disappointment. The multiple consequently edged downward until in mid-1973 the share was selling at barely above the pack—and that was before the Great Crumple.

Over time, all stocks regress or progress toward the norm. Thus Xerox, thus Beecham. Inherited intelligence does much the same thing; possibly some natural law is involved. If you do buy above the norm, your most important activity thereafter is to look out for the first sign of regression—and get out.

If you are buying *below* the norm, then sooner or later, all other things (like actually earning some profits) being equal, you can confidently expect an upward progression, whatever the market does in general.

The law of prime long-term growth is no law at all. "Prime long-term growth" is an abstraction, one of the competitive and contradictory stock market theories which can eventually lead to total withdrawal, a state characterized by remarks like, "I buy stocks because I think they are going to rise, and I sell them because I think it's time to do so, but I don't know why I do either."

Stocks like Xerox are never worth more than one thing: not what people will pay for them in the future, but what they are paying in the here and now. If they are paying a great deal today, because the shares are priced way above the market, then it is all the gold in Fort Knox against a set of dental fillings that in the none-too-distant future other investors will only pay all too little for exactly the same piece of desirable stock exchange estate.

5 Races That Go to the Swift Don't Have Many Winners

The forces that made the equity necessary in the past still exist, mainly the lack of any credible alternative for the investor who doesn't want his return fixed, and measured out only in modest quantities, from Day One.

Your alternatives to equity investment are (1) the bed (the underneath of it); (2) the superbed, or interest-bearing deposits in banks, etc.; (3) fixed interest securities, such as government bonds and loan stocks; (4) real estate; (5) things—ranging from old and young masters to diamonds to old books via objects like Staffordshire portrait figures or Japanese *netsuke*; (6) commodities, including the prince of them, which is gold.

These alternatives either lack the upward potential of the equity—the fact that you don't know where its rise, if any, will stop. Or else they don't have the prime virtue of liquidity, of easy translation into cash. Or else they need expertise that few investors can muster.

Adam Smith, the author of *The Money Game* and

Supermoney, got badly burned in hot cocoa—twice. He bought the stuff directly, and got caught by a falling market. Later he was caught by a Swiss bank which harbored a genius who was foolishly set on cornering the world cocoa market.

Art shares the problem of difficult conversion into cash—you might offer your heirloom at auction when there is a close season on Gainsborough—and it also demands both knowledge and love. If you genuinely love your Staffordshire Sir Robert Peel, your Francis Bacon screaming Pope, or your monochrome K'ang Hsi porcelain, you will sell it only in dire emergency.

That's an attitude you should never adopt with shares. Don't fall into the trap of the family quoted by the aforesaid Adam Smith, which rigidly kept through two generations to a paternal injunction never to sell their shares in IBM; they consequently became very rich but never actually had much money. Shun the state of mind that hangs onto a share year after year "because it's done me so well." People in this mental condition can even fail completely to notice that the stock long ago ceased to do anything for them at all.

Having money is the object of the exercise. You want an investment that is easy to purchase, easy to mind and easy to dispose of, both psychologically and physically. That's why the idea of the common stock, freely traded between individuals on open exchanges, is such a wonderful invention. Its basic defect is that the people who man, run and serve the exchanges make their livings, not out of the success of their customers, but out of the volume of the trade.

"Our word is our bond" (*Dictum Verbum Pactum*): that's the noble motto of London's Stock Exchange, and it will do for most others. Ring up your nearest and dearest stockbroker, ask him to buy or sell a security and you can trust him (more or less) to get the best price going, and to carry out your instructions to the letter (or thereabouts). And that's all that the exchanges promise. How did we come to expect so much more, not so much from the stock exchanges, but from the investment companies that deal with the exchanges on our behalf—at one remove, you might say?

Our conditioning by the relative security of bank accounts helps to explain our readiness to leave our wealth in the care of persons unknown. And that, like trust in pieces of paper, is a main structural foundation of the financial world. The apparent safety of the banks has helped to lull investors into a false sense of security about all variations of parting with cash in exchange for less guaranteed paper. The act of soliciting money seems to confer some respectability, just as asking bankers for an enormous loan automatically and perversely stamps the would-be borrower as a man of substance.

I have always found it hard to convince people not to place funds with dreadful little outfits whose high interest rates alone wave a red flag. Those beyond-the-fringe operators don't even have to make any special effort to attract deposits which, on all the evidence of the recent past, will be lost without trace.

Other monetary homes away from home, while respectable enough, also offer less security than the big banks. This applies to homes of long-term investment as well as short. At least the banks always give us our money back: a dollar for a dollar. Not so the insurance companies: the low surrender values and uncertain

47

yields of the insurance policy helped to open the door to practitioners who offered the same goods in a different, neater package.

The mutual fund is only an extension of the investment idea from which the insurance industry has made untold billions down the years. In both cases the fund managers invest our money as they please, charging us not only for the managerial services, but for the highly nourishing commissions paid to the salesmen who rope us in.

The mutual fund investor can take out his money (or what's left after paying often extortionate charges) at any moment he chooses. He can also learn to the last decimal point what his investment is worth at any time. What he can't do is form any idea of what it *will* be worth—though you wouldn't have guessed this from the sales talk. If the fund managers stated that 142% growth had been achieved in seven years, you couldn't blame people for supposing they were factually correct, or even for succumbing to the implied promise that 142% would be theirs, too, for the asking in the next seven years. The investor's own desire for 142% of new wealth outweighed the knowledge that birds in the bush don't always stay there.

Among the more skilled bird-in-the-bush outfits was Investors Overseas Services. When actual performance became so poor that its illusionism no longer worked, IOS turned to phantom figures—such as the notorious valuation of Alaskan land holdings at many times the purchase price on the strength of the sale of a fraction of those holdings to an intimately interested third party. This was only an advanced and conspicuous form of a species of share-pushing which followed inevitably from the axiom that the performance is the promise.

Other high performers and lofty promisers went in for eccentricities like "letter stock," whose main advantage lay in escaping the scrutiny of the Securities and Exchange Commission. Still others fell for stories taller than the Empire State Building—like the British fund operator who placed his investors' loot into a nonexistent California gold mine. The name of this fund was appropriately Surinvest, appropriate because the funds' selling pitch always lies in surety, in the promise that you can be safe, secure, sure—and rich.

Fast bucks and security don't go together. Compare mutual funds with an absolutely secure investment—lending to outfits that finance house purchase. The money is lent to citizens whose financial worthiness is attested before the loan is made. The operation is doubly secure, secured by the financial standing of the borrower, and protected by the mortgage on the property itself. Against these standards, any mutual fund investment, since it has no base in real values, is insecurity itself.

That applies equally to the mutual property investments which staged the last and briefest swelling of the Big Bubble. Performance in equity markets had become progressively more difficult to achieve. But commercial property seemed to be advancing without let or hindrance. (Literally without let: many buildings were sold more than once, each time at a luscious profit, before they ever found tenants.)

Many hucksters sold stakes in property on the mutual principle. The fund owned choice properties all over Manhattan or London or England or the globe, and the investors, so complete was their conditioning, took the operators' word for it when they alleged that such and such a skyscraper, bought for a mere $25 million, was now worth $40 million.

Each share in the fund represented a share in the hypothetical values of the properties. The greater the pressure on the fund to sell, however, the more hypothetical the value becomes. Not only do investors have to trust that past appreciation in property values will continue, they must believe that the promoters will value these baubles conservatively, and (most important) that their fellow investors will never force a sale of the assets by demanding more cash back than the fund can conveniently repay.

The collapse of offshore operations like Gramco and the Real Estate Fund of America was inevitable in the wake of the IOS crash, as other offshore investors scrambled to get back to the safety of land. The true betrayal, however, didn't lie in the fraudulence which was endemic, even inherent, in the offshore operations like IOS and Gramco. The betrayers were those, on-shore as well as off, upright as well as crooked, who went on assuring people, directly and indirectly, that they could simultaneously enjoy great safety and high profit.

The trust that was deserved by most of the respectable got extended to the disreputable partly because the latter were in cahoots with the former. Every fraudulent or quasi-fraudulent operation had trustees and bankers of impeccable pedigree, bearing and repute. The list of backers for the public offering of IOS stock reads like a Debrett of investment banking. (Their presence on that roll of honor has probably been expunged from the race memory by now.)

At best the name guaranteed solely that our money would be placed in investments after no more than a reasonable delay, and that those investments actually existed. It didn't follow that the investments were sage or sound: the trustees had no obligation to ensure that our money was administered as scrupulously as most of them invested funds entrusted to their own loving care.

Every balance sheet of a failed fund or busted company, too, had been approved by some distinguished firm of auditors. But their endorsement only meant that the books agreed with the directors' statements, and didn't conflict with reality—that reality being an elastic concept.

As the Great Crumple rumbled on, several firms of auditors in America were on the receiving end of lawsuits from shareholders who argued that the elasticity had been overdone. But in Britain, where corporate crashes were at least as numerous, every single auditor stayed safe behind the smoke screen of words and conventions which gave them fees without undue responsibility.

In the United States, the supervising authorities must take their share of the odium. In the insurance industry, not only Equity Funding, but Standard Life Corporation might as well not have been supervised for all the good that supervision did. By the time the Securities and Exchange Commission, the FBI and the U.S. attorneys got to the Standard offices, evidence had piled up (according to *Business Week*) of "twice-pledged collateral, computer fraud, executive self-dealing, forgeries, embezzlement, and stock manipulation" —and a couple of billions' worth of insurance policies were at stake here.

The cops of the investment world rely greatly on the presumed integrity of its inhabitants. But in the focal area of the Second Great Crash, the stock market, the connection between integrity and protection is at its most imperfect. The exchanges are merely markets, where the law of *caveat emptor* applies. The main exception is that, if a member firm's failure jeopardizes the holdings of its clients, the other members of the exchange will collectively come to the rescue (a principle that was strained to the point of cracking, if not beyond, by Wall Street's set of distinguished bankruptcies—the rescuers were sometimes in plights nearly as parlous as the rescued).

Stock markets exist to enable us to trade our ownership interests—a perfectly desirable purpose, but all there is to the matter. The exchanges rarely fuel the engine of industry, as they like to pretend, by providing funds. At odd times, when interest rates are high and institutional funds abound, the stock market tops up the equity funds of companies which are overborrowed or otherwise strapped for cash. At most times, compared to the largesse distributed (at a price) by the banks, by governments (hardly ever for any price at all) and by shareholders in retained cash flow (at no price in any circumstances), the stock market's money is a mere smidgen.

Like any commodity market, stock exchanges create froth, speculation, false glamour, stupidities, phony fortunes, opportunities for wrongdoing and being wrong-done, and so on. But in the years of the Big Bubble, while protesting their virtue and utility, and even while imposing tighter rules on their members and on quoted companies, the exchanges were allowing murderous excesses to develop—largely because the minds involved, as well as the machinery, were being swamped by the demand.

The cult of the equity swelled to meet an upsurge

of savings with neither parallel nor precedent. In an age in which installment debt mushroomed to heights that terrified conservatives, people also saved in colossal quantities. As the average Western man grew richer, so his savings piled up, not necessarily his private nest egg, but all the various forms of collective savings as well—the pension fund, the insurance policy, and so on. Simply placing this Niagara of billions is a giant problem. The world's governments can absorb much of the money, but there are limits to the size of their borrowings, the national debts; equally, there are strict bounds to the amounts that can go into private house finance, or into fixed interest loans to industry. The stock market provides a perfect out.

Money pumped into equities goes nowhere else. When we invest in stock markets we merely exchange one piece of paper (currency) for another (stock)—and in most cases the currency isn't put to any purpose by the company that issued the shares in the first place. There is no finite limit to the amount that equity markets can absorb—so long as the price of stocks and shares is free to rise.

At this point a benevolent circle begins to revolve. As the market moves ahead, spurred by our money seeking investment, so the valuation of the market (what it would cost to buy all the stocks in which it trades) becomes larger, expanding its apparent ability to absorb still more money. Moreover, the decision of investors and investing institutions to buy common stock is justified by the same token—the prices of stocks are rising, so we must have been brilliantly right to buy stocks, and to shun (relatively speaking) bonds.

As late as August 1975, AAA-rated corporate bonds, at 8.9%, gave twice as much yield as Wall Street stocks.

This wasn't because the riskiness of common stocks had been removed by some suspension of the laws of business economics; it was because fixed interest stocks are fully and alarmingly exposed to the double villains of the New Economic Age—taxation and inflation.

The equity gave apparent protection on both counts. In the first place, the company didn't need to pay a dividend if the management and the stockholders didn't want it paid. The profits could be kept in the business, free of personal income tax, to be reinvested to produce still more profits. The price of the shares would rise to reflect this mounting profit—and you could pocket your proceeds as capital gains, taxed at the lower rate.

As inflation ran ahead, profits would automatically be inflated, too, and the share price would rise in step with inflation. Nor was that the only insurance: behind the price of the stock stood the assets, which plainly became worth more in current money with every fresh twist in the inflationary spiral.

Almost nobody recognized that this argument was the economic equivalent, intellectually speaking, of fool's gold. In the harsh reality of economics, high security tends to go with low yield, and *vice versa*. But only some of the people were greedy enough to ignore this law, or to believe that it could be repealed for their especial benefit. The majority were probably happy to settle for a cash depository that would preserve their capital in real terms and provide, over the long run, a reasonable return on the money, after tax.

After allowing for the tax on capital gains, that humble ambition might have meant a total rise over two mildly inflationary (3% a year) decades of around 400%, or something short of 8½% per annum compound. As a matter of hard historical fact, relatively few of the stocks proudly listed on the world's exchanges managed this feat—and that's a *minimal* standard.

The race, in other words, went only to the very swift, of whom there were, by definition, very few. The search for gold amid the surrounding also-rans was bound to lead to unbridled lust for weird and wonderful stocks. Perhaps the weirdest of these wonders was a computer services stock which differed from all the others by actually making a profit. The other computer stocks, when they came to market, were all happily in loss, which made their price-earnings ratios infinite, whereas the price-earnings ratio for the newcomer was in triple figures. When the prospectus for this superior offering was published on Wall Street, the investing institutions that had subscribed for the issue promptly dumped it.

Even sophisticated investors must act irrationally when they rest their policy on substantially beating the norm. They are like the man who presses a button in the knowledge that, half the time, a moderately valuable red ball will pop out of the box. The rest of the time will be equally divided between the appearance of a money-losing black ball and a rich gold one. Yet knowing this, the man consistently bets on the appearance of gold. For every once that he comes up gold, he must get two reds and one money-losing black number.

The average performance of stock markets around the world produced too little gold to live up to the billing of the equity cult. But those who sold us our equity investments were most unwilling to face this unwelcome fact. Instead, they sought other explanations. In

1973, as the slide gathered momentum, they could blame all manner of outside mayhem: the world monetary crisis, the deepening shadow and stain of Nixon's Watergate and Götterdämmerung, and some scandals of rare juiciness even by Wall Street standards —such as the monstrous Equity Funding affair.

Coming on top of massive thefts of stock certificates, this $100 million swindle, which involved the issue of phony insurance policies—over sixty-four thousand of which didn't exist—and the certifying of imaginary deaths of fictitious people, didn't fortify wavering faith either in an economy built on trusted pieces of paper, or in the cult of the uncommon common stock.

When the market rallied in 1975, rising by a third in no time at all, the professionals quickly resurfaced. But this phenomenon was at least initially different from earlier celebrations of the cult: the reaction against the past worship was so severe that common stocks had become truly cheap—as opposed to the spurious cheapness of the past. Once again, the investors, you and I, were in with a hope.

6 If the Hare Lies Down, Ride the Tortoise

When performance was in flower, many and wondrous were the theories for making sure mints from markets. For instance, we could put our faith in computers, which supposedly could outcalculate Einstein and Newton put together—and digest more information about the stock markets than a million analysts beavering away for a hundred years.

At the other extreme, we could pick the man rather than the machine, opting for some wizard of the market, like Manhattan's once-celebrated Chinese-American Gerald Tsai. He translated stunning success at Fidelity Capital Fund into the knockout launch in 1966 of the Manhattan Fund with $247 million of other people's money. Such men seemingly didn't need a system to set the welkin ringing—the mere touch of the Midas did the trick.

We could pick technical analysis, or chartism, in which the behavior of the market was reduced to lines and patterns on graph paper. If that seemed too mechanistic, we could select several methods by which high-performing shares could be picked out, like sixpences from a Christmas pudding, from the surrounding stodge; if that seemed too hazardous, then we could favor stocks with high asset backing, or high yields, or high cash flow per share. Name it, and it was on offer—and it always worked.

The terrible truth is that in soaring markets all theories work; in sinking markets, no theory succeeds—and no Midas touch produces gold, either. Tsai's funds soared in boom years: in 1968, when Tsai did his shrewdest deed by selling out for $30 million, the Manhattan Fund slumped as markets turned against his style. But no expert will ever confess to the boom-bust truth, because it reduces his own claims to expertise.

Yet any test of the aces usually shows that they are neither more nor less reliable than racehorse tipsters; that is, their success is no more than random—which happens to be how, according to the highly respectable academic theory of the "Random Walk," stock markets do behave.

The theory holds that share prices fluctuate in random fashion around a price which is the intrinsic or underlying value of the stock. This begs the big question of what can possibly be the intrinsic value in a price determined by market forces, but this large quibble is insignificant against the results of a test conducted by a computer at the Chicago Graduate School of Business. It chose at random 56.5 million buying and selling transactions on the New York Stock Exchange. It wound up with a median rate of return of 9.8% annually. Its chance of achieving a profit was not only better than three out of four, but also far better than the results of following the nonrandom choice of the typical expert.

If the Hare Lies Down, Ride the Tortoise

No better proof of this accusation exists than the experience of a group of Wall Street veterans who gather each year for a "pre-Christmas luncheon and a Christmas list of favorite stocks." The words are from *Newsweek*, which made its readers privy to the menu at the Christmas 1972 beanfeast. The point is not so much the 1973 tips but the blithe way in which the veterans sailed ahead undeterred by the record of the previous festivities.

They had tipped twenty-three stocks, of which thirteen had fallen between lunches. Of the remaining ten, only eight managed to grow by more than the Dow Jones index. The veterans would have lost half their money on two of the twenty-three and made 50% or more on only four. Yet 1972 wasn't one of the horror-show years to come. The market had actually risen by 13.6% since the veterans had last tasted Christmas pudding. Had the convivial old-timers invested in all twenty-three stocks the average gain would have been 7%, or about half the rise recorded by the market as a whole. Counsel for the defense could begin by saying that these are about the right odds for an investor in search of what *Newsweek*'s Clem Morgello calls the "big winners"—the company, often little-known or temporarily out of favor, that promises to catch fire and race ahead in a short period of time by half or more.

That kindly judgment only proves that the quest for big winners is a mug's game in the first place, and that these veterans, who are no different in this respect than any other Wall Street group you care to pick, are no better at the game than you would expect a mug to be.

Potential "big winners" are better named "maybe" stocks. To take the veterans' list as an illustration, *maybe* the Wankel engine was going to make it big (it did, briefly enough, and so in 1972 did Curtiss-Wright, which had a license on the invention). *Maybe* Leasco, the computer leasing empire, would climb up off the canvas, on which it had been deposited by a number of untowards events, including the collapse of computer leasing.

The biggest *maybe* in the bunch was National Patent Development, which caught the eye of the experts because it was deep into the soft contact lens caper. But the soft product ran into the red, and the shares, in a Wall Street term of peculiar beatitude, "headed South." They ended the year off 61.3%, a fair way toward the Antarctic, after having been 95.6% to the good at one point.

Here beginneth the second defense. With fireball or *maybe* shares, you must know when to head, not South, but homeward. The veterans pointed out that the average gain of their Christmas selections from lunchtime onward to the 1972 highs was almost 62%, compared to only 16.7% for the Dow Jones index. But this defense, one which stock market tipsters love, will never wash. It represents the purest mountain water of hindsight.

The tipster is saying that, *if* you had known when each stock was going to peak, you would have come out splendidly ahead of the game, and that is as hypothetical as an *if* can get. It postulates perfect timing, which is all but impossible with one stock, let alone with twenty-three. It compares, moreover, the peaks of these selected stocks, all reached at different dates in the year, with the level of a market index (which is arrived at by averaging the peaks, lows and in-betweens of a totally unselected group of stocks) on just one day in 1972.

To add one other maybe to the list, *maybe*, if the Dow Jones constituent stocks had been measured from Christmas Eve to *their* respective individual peaks, a better gain than 60% would have been achieved—and there are precious few fireballs, "big winners" or hot stocks in the Dow Jones.

Any group, asked on Christmas Eve to name an individual stock that will cover itself and themselves with glory for the whole of the ensuing twelve months, is likely to come ingloriously unstuck. Failure is the name of this particular game, because the exercise flies in the face of the essence of markets, *which is to fluctuate and to be illogical*.

There is an old and valuable truth about fine wine: there are no good wines, only good bottles. By the same token, there are no good buys in shares, only good sales. If you sell a share for more than you paid, the buy was good. If not, not. But the tipster operates on the comfortable thesis that there are no bad tips, only good ones: the bad ones he forgets about, on the general line that the good that men do (in the stock market, at least) lives after them, while the evil is interred with its own bones.

This is beauteously illustrated by the chartist. Studying his "heads and shoulders," "base areas," "upside projections," "reversal patterns," "top areas" and other graphical joys, the chartist will advise that a certain stock is set to head from, say, 167 to 264. If it fails to do so, sliding perhaps to 130, the chartist is not the least bit abashed. The pattern, he will confidently report, has "aborted."

Anybody who claims, like the Wall Street vets, that a bad tip was really magnificent, because you could have sold at a profit, had you only know when, cannot retire behind the excuse; he must produce evidence that he actually advised the customers to sell at the peak.

Moreover, if you deal in fireballs, and only count their gains to the peak, you are cooking the books in another respect—any fireball that does explode may travel so fast and far that it outweighs the indifference of the rest of the pack. No less than a quarter of the 60% gain which the Wall Street choices showed from their Christmas price to their respective peaks came from one stock: Curtiss-Wright, with its license on the Wankel engine wonder. It finished the year up 172%. Without this one star performer, the entire portfolio of hot tips would have shown a year-on-year gain of precisely nothing.

The cult of performance, however, forces the expert to choose hot stocks rather than cool performers: the public of the bubble period was woefully unimpressed by safe and solid selections. In one exercise carried out in 1973, two random selections of stocks were pitted against each other, in a stock market replay of Aesop's race between the tortoise and the hare. The tortoise stocks were rich with asset value, high in dividend yield and deep in defensive qualities. The hares, in contrast, were all selling at the astronomic multiples of earnings which designated a high-performance growth stock.

The results were predictable. While neither portfolio resisted the Second Great Crash, the tortoises were slower going down than the hares, a third of which disappeared off the bottom altogether. Yet every single hare had been vigorously backed by the investment experts; hence their soaring PE ratios.

At a London dinner meeting similar to the Wall Street Christmas luncheon, the tortoise and hare philosophies came into direct conflict. The tortoise was a dreary, old, family sugar company, Tate & Lyle, best known for its implacable objections to being nationalized. The hare was Associated Dairies, a milk firm that had arisen like a meteor by its success in promoting American-style superstores in the nether reaches of England.

The diners overwhelmingly rejected slow and steady sugar in favor of fast milk, convinced by a merchant banker's eloquent testimony to the brilliance and depth of Asda's management, and the dazzling scope of its growth potential. There was nothing wrong in this analysis except that it totally misread the future of the shares. As the Great Crash bottomed out, the sugar company was selling at about the same price as the day of the dinner. The superstore hare had fallen by two-thirds.

In bear markets, as a general rule, the "defensive" stock does better than the aggressive one—just as, when the action roars away, the aggressors make the running. But many expert advisers never observe this fundamental rule of markets, nor any other of the ancient reliable rules of thumb which substitute experience for inspiration.

As their customers, we were in an uncertain state of mind, anyway. Most of us had grasped the rule that, the higher the interest, the greater the risk of the investment; but in the stock market the reverse may be true—the high-yield stocks may very well be safer than the one with a virtually invisible dividend return on the purchase price. Many were unable to make this psychological transition—especially since the high-yield stocks either were "dogs," or were valued as such, while the low-yield ones were "highfliers" and therefore obviously desirable.

The resulting confusion achieved a neglect of first principles in investment: as investors bought "growth," past and projected, instead of the dividends which were the only reality, so their actions, and the reflections of those actions in share prices, became further and further removed from the bases of investment.

This placed the expert himself in an invidious position. Even if he realized that such fundamentals as the relationship of bond yields to equity yields still had to rule at the end of the day, markets were being swayed in the meantime by other considerations entirely, such as the potential for soft contact lenses.

In 1973 the Wall Street lunchers showed more interest in large, badly bombed companies like American Motors (a hardy perennnial in such lists), Chrysler, Reynolds and Westinghouse. They also found a peculiarly delectable railroad, the Providence and Worcester, whose total network of track is precisely forty-one miles.

But the authentic flavor of their selection was better conveyed by stocks like Alpex Computer, which hadn't made a profit in its life, but which *maybe* would someday. (Alpex has since disappeared off the face of the stock market.) There was also Soundesign, which made hi-fi equipment and minicomputers—in those familiar bulwarks of the U.S. economy, Japan and Taiwan. And for the second year in a row, they chose National Patent

Development, soft contact lenses and all, though the year before the stock had ended 61.3% off.

Now, it seemed, the lens problems were sorted out, and a mouthwash and a dental chemical were thrown in for luck. It didn't do any good: NPD and Soundesign ended up in early 1975 in exactly the same place as in 1972, with prices that left plenty of change from a $10 bill.

Over the years of guessing wrong about the unguessable, pundits like our Wall Street friends learn that they cannot afford to be without two hands—on the one hand this, on the other that. This Delphic device keeps their necks where they should be: not sticking out. But psychology, and the need to encourage the customers to buy, dictates that it is safer, hand-wise, to ride with the crowd when the market is rising. When it is falling, contrariwise, the two hands dictate that silence is the best policy. That leaves you with the mental difficulty (but the necessary task) of accepting that experts truly know no more about which stock will rise and which fall, than you do.

7 Too Many Cooks Spoil the Market

We all love the myth that a crock of gold lies at the end of the rainbow. There simply has to be a better way of earning a living than filling teeth, writing books, building houses or driving a cab in New York City. Moreover, a few fortunates do find crocks of gold at the end of their personal rainbows, and none of us wants to accept that our own golden dreams will never come true.

History's pages are splattered by glittering bubbles, of many different shapes and sizes, blown up by this desire of the many to copy the few. The gambling fever is another example of this nearly universal addiction. Gamblers in the mass always lose—otherwise the organizers would never make their cut, the profit—yet the gambler must believe that he may be the exception who wins.

The strangest form of gamble is where the speculator knows that he must always lose—or, rather, where the figures show that he must. These oddities include the stroke of perverse genius that built a whole new school of business in the sixties: the exchange of paper, of common stock or its cunning variations, for the assets and earnings of another company.

The first creative use of acquisitions antedated the new conglomerates of the sixties by several decades. Nearly all the between-wars corporate mammoths owed at least part of their growth, even their existence, to mergers. But these deals were not motivated by the stock market: General Motors and Unilever, General Foods and Royal Dutch-Shell, and so on, merged for mighty economic motives, from eliminating powerful competition to defense against competitors who were too powerful to be eliminated.

These practitioners mostly failed to exploit the opportunity that had attracted J. P. Morgan to mergers. Morgan, in an age of lax regulation and morals, deluged the public with watered stock. If you sell more in shares than a company is actually worth, you pocket the extra proceeds; but the price of those shares will fall toward that lower underlying value—not because stock markets possess any intrinsic sense of values, but because the balance sheet has been hideously weakened and the supply of the stock greatly increased.

Stock markets, like all markets, are only moved at the margin. If demand for 1000 tons of copper is met by a potential supply of 1100 tons, that will sharply reduce the price. If the supply falls to 900 tons, however, the price must swing rapidly upward, as the customers for the missing 100 tons outbid each other for the stuff. Demand (or usage) has remained more or less constant throughout this commotion, as you would expect with a commodity that industry has to use. But nobody "uses" or needs to buy a stock or share—and that produces a crucial perversion.

The entry into commodity markets of people who have no more personal use for copper than a vegetarian has for steak tartare can pervert these markets in a similar way. When a shortfall in supply pushes up the copper price, speculators will buy solely because its price is rising. The idea of actually taking delivery—getting a small mountain of metal off-loaded on their front lawns —would horrify them. By moving in on the action, however, the speculators drive the price higher still.

By the same token, if the price drops, the gamblers will dive off the high board—because they only climbed up in the first place in the expectation of a further rise. The balance of real supply and true demand determines the overall pattern of the market, but the impact of speculation distorts that pattern in both directions— up and down.

You can see why the use of paper to buy earnings had a built-in disadvantage: it automatically increased the supply of the shares. The ace conglomerators sought to postpone this black day by issuing funny money shares, or warrants, or letter stock, which would only be added to the supply of genuine equity at some later date. But investment analysts were perfectly capable of working out the company's sums on the relevant basis: what its earnings per share would be if fully diluted—when all the comical paper was converted into serious stock certificates.

The device was as useless as garlic in averting the evil eye. The amount of claims on the company's earnings was still being increased faster than the desire of the investment community to share in those claims. The problem (barely seen as such even by the cleverest promoters) was compounded by a defect which will always cripple mergermongers. This flaw is the Law of

Diminishing Amalgamation Returns—the fact that the impact of a $1-million-a-year purchase on a $2-million company is twice as great as its effect on a $4-million concern.

What's more, companies that consist of several ill-assorted interests have never been loved by investors. This isn't difficult to square with the soaring prices of conglomerates shares. Their high flight resulted not from high valuation, but from the rocket-booster effect of large injections of earnings into a tiny vehicle. Even if the price-earnings multiple never got above a miserable 10 (and a conglomerate like Gulf + Western sometimes sold even in the heady days at less than that), earnings growth of 40%, 50% or 70% a year was bound to translate into a leaping share price.

The progenitors and public relations men of these creations strove their utmost to engineer escape into the higher atmosphere in which spaceships like Xerox and Polaroid spun at their magic price-earnings multiples. But efforts to escape the conglomerate tag (via public relations euphemisms like "multimarket corporation") couldn't raise the public's limited enthusiasm for this kind of investment vehicle. In any event, as we have noted, the promoters of Textron or Litton, Gulf + Western or Ling-Temco-Vought, Bangor Punta or ITT were pushing a rock uphill—their efforts to promote the shares were constantly offset by their equally consistent increase in the supply of that paper.

The acquisition artist can avoid the problem by using debt. Buy earnings for less than the interest charges on the debt, and the result flows straight through to the reported profits—even under honest accounting. But this adds a fresh and well-known hazard to the risks of buying a rotten apple.

The device of "gearing" or leverage is older than the joint stock company itself. Accountancy conventions mean that, if two companies have identical profits, but one has half its capital in the form of debt, the latter will have higher earnings per share than the one that is debt-free—provided, again, that its overall return on capital exceeds the rate of interest on the debt—and it may well command a higher rating.

This may sound like rank rubbish to you: how can a debt-laden company be rated lower than a concern that owes not one red cent? Surely the correct valuation would be the other way about. As so often, the simple observation is right. The supposedly sophisticated are wrongly impressed not just by the high per share earnings of the indebted, highly "leveraged" company, but by the awesome impact of any improvement in profits.

If a company with $10 million of equity capital raises its $1 million profits to $1.5 million, that's a spiffing 50% rise—but that's all. Now: if the firm has $5 million of equity and $5 million of debt and the debt costs 10% a year in interest, the original $1 million of profit will be scaled down by the interest charges to $500,000. But the returns on the equity capital will be identical. The same half-million increase in profit mentioned above, moreover, will raise the profit to $1 million without any rise in the interest costs. That means profits will *double*, and the return on stockholders' equity, 10% before the profit rise (the same as for the debt-free case), will now be a full 20% (against 15% for the debtless company).

Move into the higher realms of 90% gearing, and a $100,000 profit gets transmuted into a sixfold increase by the same simple alchemy. The ugly reverse side of this beautiful coin is known to any investor who has ever invested unwisely with borrowed money—every investor, for instance, who got wiped out in the First Great Crash.

To revert to our examples, the debt-free dullard could withstand a $1 million fall in profits and still pay a 5% dividend. The same fall leaves the switched-on borrower switched off: his 50% gearing means he would just cover his interest costs—and nothing will be left for the shareholders. The blazing genius who had jacked his debt up to 90% would be deep in the black hole of Calcutta: profits wiped out, and short by $400,000 of the $900,000 owed in interest charges.

The paper-for-earnings wheeler-dealers of the sixties sailed between Scylla and Charybdis: if they used debt, they were wide open to the perils of gearing-in-reverse. If they used equity, they ran into potential double-trouble.

The first trap was increasing the supply of shares faster than the demand. A company like ITT, increasing the number of common shares outstanding from 41 million to 96 million between 1966 and 1972, was doing more than expecting a 129% rise in the amount of investor interest in its shares, for the object of the whole exercise was to elevate the price per share, too.

But the act of exchanging equity for other companies' earnings had the inevitable effect of making the stock less lovable to the investing public in case after case. There were two extremes. The company could buy another firm at a lower price-earnings ratio than its own, which was the way in which the conglomerates were supposed to earn their keep. Or it could buy stock at a higher multiple than its own—which, more often than not, was how the wizards actually behaved.

A painstaking article in *Fortune* magazine revealed this curious habit. Few episodes were as bizarre as Gulf + Western's purchase of Paramount at a 70 multiple when its own stock was selling at only 8. But the general conclusion was clear. The conglomerates grew by deals that had precisely the same effect as purchasing earnings with borrowed money for prices so high that the bought-in profits would not cover the debt interest.

The only possible logic behind this paradoxical behavior arose if (which, mainly thanks to *The Godfather* I and II, actually happened with Paramount) the earnings of the acquired company could be jacked up sharply and in short order. But for all their self-alleged management skills, this was a feat that few conglomerates could contrive. It's a feat, in fact, which few managements pull off with consistency.

The upshot was to turn a lying boast into reality. The overlords of Litton Industries, for instance, used to repel critics with arguments that half their growth had been organic—that is, derived from expansion of the original businesses, rather than simply bought in. (It sounds much less good, somehow, to assert, with equal truth, that half of a company's growth is the result of acquisitions.)

But self-styled supermanagers like Litton's were anxious to establish an image of themselves as more than just pretty stock market faces, as managers who could have flourished just as richly (well almost) if the market had never existed. In fact, it often turned out to be perfectly true that their earnings performance, and presumably their stock market rating, would have been higher if, after the initial setup by acquisition, the promoters had forbidden themselves all further purchases.

The statement applies even where the purchaser applied the traditional leverage, using a highly rated stock to buy a lowly one. On the face of it, a company can't lose by swapping paper that values earnings at a multiple of 40, say, for paper valuing the selfsame dollars at 20. But look at it from the purchased stockholder's point of view. There you were with stock priced at 15, for example, and of little interest to anybody (which is why it was priced so low). Then along comes some hairy ape of a conglomerate and offers you a third above the market price.

It is exactly as if, having sold his holding for cash, the shareholder in the acquired company had been offered shares by the bidding company at a discount. True—but won't the *bidding* shareholders think it worth paying over the odds? After all, they (through the agency of their aggressive, farsighted managers) are giving away mere pieces of paper for valuable earnings. If the market values the new earnings as highly as the old, the worth of those earnings in the share price will be double the sum actually expended, and everybody will live happily ever after.

But what happens if the market changes its view of the stock? Buying an extra $200,000 of earnings for a $1 million company, if the latter is valued in the stock market at $40 million, raises the equity's market worth to $48 million—if the price-earnings multiple holds. But the potential loss of market worth if the multiple declines only to 30 will wipe out all the benefit—and more. For the "new" shareholders, the $4 million they received will then only be worth $3 million. For the "old" shareholders, the $40 million with which they started out will swiftly shrink in the wash to $33 million.

Why on earth, or on Wall Street, should the

multiple shrink? There are two main mundane reasons. Apart from the worsening of the supply-demand relationship which is risked by enlarging the equity, there's the unpleasant truth that the new shareholders are more likely than the old to sell their stock. Enough of those desertions, and the price must inevitably, obeying the laws of all markets, head downward. The tobogganing seldom happens overnight—although there was a sickening overnight slip in Rank Organisation shares when Wall Street investors reacted savagely to the news that the company foolishly wanted to buy a brewery.

But that Wall Street reaction came in a later, better-instructed period, when investors had learned that the paper-for-earnings trick rested on the most shifting of all financial ground—a market valuation. The take-over is in effect a fund-raising operation, in which the cash is used to buy an additional business. If the return on that purchase is greater than that on the original capital, then the purchasing company has been strengthened, at least for the time being. If not, a drag has been created on further progress.

None of these sad thoughts disturbed the merry merchants in earnings in the sixties. As they wheeled and dealed, they and the conventional wisdom expected the mere announcement of a new earnings caper to boost the price of both victim and aggressor.

Yet a standard procedure in such cases was to arrange a little friendly support for the prices until the deal went through. If the operation was so wealth-enhancing for the shareholders, how come the market needed propping up—not to mention cooking?

It is small comfort to know that many chefs of this particular market dish in the end got thoroughly cooked themselves. The greater comfort lies in the contemplation of conventional wisdom and its disasters. Conventional wisdom represents the ideas foisted on us by leaders who can only see what is in front of their noses. The truly wise individual looks backward as well as forward to find and profit from the unconventional truth.

8 The Pursuit of Glory
Leads But to the Grave

The shares that made the headlines and the money in the sixties had one general characteristic: the purchasers, however briefly, esteemed the qualities of the managements. That respect was often greater if the management, to the naked eye, consisted of only one man. Genius in management, like genius in art, but for less good reason, is commonly held to be at its best when undiluted by the presence of others. Those who backed a Ross Perot in computer services, a Charlie Bluhdorn in conglomerates, a Bernie Cornfeld in mutual funds, did so without knowing or caring about the quality of the minions. Enough that a maestro was on the podium: he could be trusted to hire a good orchestra, or at least to make it play in financial tune.

In a sense, those who took the maestro's eye view were reverting to the days when business was thought of in terms of men rather than management. Only after the Second World War did the pioneering work in organization and methods blossom into the modern school of management.

As the level of organizational expertise rose postwar, as the numbers trained in management theory grew, and as the output of that theory increased, so the idea gradually gained currency that management was like a company's technological resources: an identifiable asset, part of the firm's basic strength.

The problem is that management consists almost entirely of men. They cannot be inspected or judged like a set of blueprints. True, the men have methods —like, say, the famous decentralized organization of General Motors. But the methods are inseparable from the men, and nobody knows how to separate the contribution of methodology from the other strengths: like the sales network bequeathed by corporate ancestors, or the technological resources which can last out two or three generations of top management.

Still, the statement that a GM, or a Shell, or a Du Pont, or a Boeing has superior management is safe enough. Holding these complex operations together demands high organizational skills, and the pressure for high skills, together with the grandeur of the jobs, attracts the finest organization men: recruits whom the biggest corporations can pay the highest rewards.

But investors are not attracted by this proposition —probably with justice. The extra management qualities of the giant are offset, often outweighed, by the solidifying effects of bureaucracy and the other constipations that come with large scale. Only if you seek safety will you turn to the big blue-chip: although your sole security is that the business won't go bankrupt and will rise (but also fall) with the economic cycle. If you want to sample the joys of dynamic management, you turn elsewhere.

But if this is your bag, you aren't really seeking qual-

77

ity of management, you're seeking the *results* of "good" management. It follows that managers are judged solely by their results, and up to a point, this is just. After all, no manager can claim prowess without performance. But the linkage breaks at the point where results are identified with managerial brilliance.

Consider two men throwing unloaded dice. A backer wants his man to come up with the winning number more times, but he wouldn't conclude that the winner is actually more physically skilled at throwing dice. The success of managements may have as little to do with innate skills; luck and timing play as much part as brilliance, and science a definitely smaller role than hunch.

In any event, since giant corporations, by virtue or vice of their size, couldn't produce the results the gamblers wanted, the latter turned to the second, third and fourth ranks; and wherever they found performance, they also proclaimed managerial brilliance. In some cases this error did actual harm to the managers themselves, if some mediocre bunch fell in love with their own false image and proceeded to ruin a respectable business. That's how the sound timber firm of Boise Cascade was turned into one of the dizziest and most disastrous seekers after conglomerate glory.

But the main result was to accentuate both the positive and the negative. The myth of management expertise first pushed the price of the shares higher; then, when the discovery of gross failures in financial control, or of fatal product obsolescence, or of some other unsuspected ailment was made, the resulting devaluation was all the sharper for the past exaggeration.

The science of management was reinforced, not just by each year's output of business school graduates, but also by the public relations effort on behalf of great national programs in aerospace. The technology of landing men on the moon was breathtaking, and outsiders assumed that equally stunning scientific applications of management underlay the technological achievement—and furthermore that skills developed in organizations like NASA could be applied with equal impact to civilian firms.

Defense contractors argued that their specific skills in military programs were not limitations, but golden opportunities. Companies emerged whose main offering was simply management. Their promoters said that since outstanding performance stemmed from superb management, a company manned entirely by scientifically trained and superbly competent managers was bound to perform superbly, to land men on the corporate moon, even though mission control hadn't decided in which business or businesses the performance would be achieved. Their business wasn't business: it was *management*. And the object of management was not to manufacture goods, or market them, or provide services; it was to produce earnings per share, and to multiply them so rapidly that the share price would quite inevitably perform with the exact precision of that first flight to the moon. And because the company was oriented entirely to management and earnings growth, the forward motion could be expected to be perpetual. Since the supermanagers were not attached to any one business or market, they would know when and how to switch when prospects dimmed.

Every article of this faith was moonshine. Management can't be separated from specific markets and businesses, educated skills can't be universally applied, a permanent corporation can't be built on shifting sands. But the most dangerous error, because it carried into traditional business, was the identification of management with financial results: specifically, earnings per share.

Pride alone inspired managements to prove (if they could) that they were just as skilled at managing as the sweetest young thing in conglomerates. They accepted the criteria which the latter had laid down: they agreed that maximizing capital gains for the stockholder was the true task of management. And they adopted the methods of the conglomerators: the search was on for diversification, for high-growth industries, for financially oriented central direction.

The disease infected, staid, solid Middle West companies were like Honeywell, which grafted onto itself a horrendously expensive computer operation that transformed the whole nature of the corporation, without contributing much in most years, save an unsustainable elevation of the price-earnings ratio into the upper 40s.

At Honeywell, the objective of the corporation became something that its founder, a single-minded salesman who used to sit in a buggy at the end of the road supervising the troops as they peddled his heating controls, would not remotely have understood: a 15% rise in earnings per share, year in and year out. The rationale was that a 15% growth company would surely always command a substantial price-earnings ratio, which would with equal certainty produce a handsome share price and capital appreciation.

The irrationality lies in the fact that, while management has many identifiable functions, none of them (outside the specialized area of the corporate finances) has any direct, immediate connection with this financial goal. Given that the connection between earnings performance and the stock price is wholly indeterminate, there is no way in which the earnings-conscious management can guarantee the results on which it sets its collective heart.

A strong or good management can achieve a variety of concrete objectives: it can avoid or eliminate no-hope, loss-making situations; it can develop to the maximum attainable potential the sound businesses in which it's engaged; it can avoid investments (diversifications or otherwise) that overstretch its resources of money and management; it can stay alert to changes in its markets that demand changes in products and practices; it can look for opportunities within its competence that will return large and early amounts on shareholders' funds; it can ensure that its subordinates and replacements are of the necessary caliber; it can keep the company's products and processes up-to-date —and so on.

All or any of these attainments will very probably have the effect of improving the company's earnings. The exceptions, however, are very important: for instance, when a company has to bunch heavy investment into one year, earnings necessarily take a beating. At crucial moments like this, the pursuit of earnings as the prime objective of the company ceases to make sense, and may impose dangerous nonsense, like the various formulas that company after company adopted to keep current expenditure on research and development out of the accounts.

Investors, even if they noticed such devices, probably didn't care. After all, if the object is to elevate earnings, how can any means that achieves that end, even a stroke of pure accountancy, be anything but great? Similarly, shutting down a loss-maker, if it demanded a large write-off, might seem less appealing than simply allowing the losses to continue and hoping that they could be stemmed, or (by some miracle) turned into profits. Time and again, the imperative of a fixed target for earnings growth was translated into an unrealistic figure not only for divisions that were in the leaky boats, but also for others in well-found vessels.

Some conglomerate operations developed a new form of business cycle. The new man arriving for the normal three-year stint as chief divisional executive would find a mess: a sharply declining profit trend, the result of inadequate investment in the previous reign. In his first year, the new man remedied the deficiencies and took the losses in profit on his predecessor's departed chin. The second year showed the inevitable sharp upturn, earning the incumbent praise and pay. But progress could only be kept going in the third year by cutting back on investment and other supporting expenditure, which meant, of course, that after the new man had been promoted, or had moved out of the conglomerate altogether to take a striking new job, his successor found himself in exactly the same mess in turn.

Another damaging process is illustrated by a case in which a profit forecast, instrumental in averting an unwelcome raid on the company, was missed by a grotesque margin. The company was organized into divisions, each with its own subsidiaries, the standard form of organization in the postwar school of management. When the forecast was drawn up, each subsidiary boss added 20% to his original budgeted profit. The division added all the forecasts together and, not to be outdone, added its 20% on top. And the central management added 20% on top of that. This geometrical progression guaranteed total disaster: by the time the original one-fifth boost had been subjected to this treatment, the group had transformed it into a 72.8% target. And there was the further absurdity in this case, as in countless others, of insistence on a particular time-span, and a twelve months' one at that.

If you are making a short-term bet, then it might make sense from your investing viewpoint to crowd all possible profits into (and defer all possible expenditures out of) the year immediately ahead. But most investors, especially the big institutions, have much longer time horizons. In 1965, a pension fund might have been predominantly interested in the outcome in 1985, when its policyholders would cash in their chips. Besides, sacrificing the long run for the short is maniacal, since, by the nature of things, the process must come to an end. The deferred expenditures will catch up with the overstated profits, and the result is a Penn Central.

The real manager has to manage for the long term. A good company (the kind in which most of us want to place our money) is a long-running attraction, which means that management decisions taken in any one year must be weighed against the long-term as well as the short-run interests of the corporation. Many of the projects essential to a company's development take a long time to mature, longer than the three years of a conglomerate job-changer, at any rate. Earnings matter to the real manager, partly as a measure of his real attainments, partly because they finance his future corporate growth. As ends in themselves, the financial targets are meaningless.

Another trap lay waiting for the manager seduced by the new blandishments. If the company was going to be valued solely on its future growth, the tendency was to forget to a damaging extent about its present levels of performance.

Suppose that two identical companies with stockholders' equity of $100 million start off from the same base date, one earning $10 million and the other $20 million, but the first growing by 15% annually and the second by 10%. Even if those relative growth rates are guaranteed to remain constant, which cannot be promised by God or man, after ten years the first company would be generating $40.5 million of profits and the latter, $51.8 million. The first firm would have been able to congratulate itself solely on moving from relatively hopeless to comparatively moderate. Its *relative* performance, and therefore its management competence, would be worse all along the line. As an indication of efficiency, its faster growth rate is meaningless.

Possibly the greatest error and most dangerous management trap lies in the concept of glory itself. Business is a splendid occupation, a worthy way of spending a career and the foundation of the modern economy. But true management is an inglorious activity, compounded of equal parts of caution and dash, of unremitting attention to detail as well as the ability to stand back and survey the panorama, of awareness of public reaction to the company's deeds and of indifference to transient signs of that reaction—such as, for main instance, the price-earnings ratio of the equity. Once the manager puts the transient first, he is doomed: each and every action, from an otiose purchase of another company to an overoptimistic forecast about a new business venture, can be justified by the possible beneficial effect it will have on the company's standing in the stock market.

But the path of cause and effect in the market

follows no known route. Nor is the short-term boost ever translated into the long-term gain. Managers who chased the share price were pursuing a chimera, and those of us who chased managements dedicated to financial growth were equally hot after a will-o'-the-wisp. Good management is something that you only recognize when you've got it, and that may never be reflected— if you are lucky—in a supreme price-earnings ratio.

9 What's Sauce for the Gander Is Zilch for the Goose

Whether or not it was good for stockholders, workers or the company itself to maximize earnings per share, it was unquestionably good for managers with a vested interest in the share price: good, that is, as long as investors would pay fanciful premiums for rapid growth in the magic numeral. The fortunes made by stock option fat cats are vast.

Even in the awful conditions of 1974, four executives in U.S. companies that reported one-year option gains cashed in $500,000 or more of personal pretax profits. The year before, according to McKinsey figures, five had million-dollar option gains. True, the number exercising options had fallen by 1974: down one-third in 1973, 55% from 1972, and leaving a mere 165 executives with their fingers in the gravy.

Shareholders were expected to rejoice in these arrangements on the old routine of sauce for goose = sauce for gander. The more the stock price soared, the more the options were worth; but since the shareholders' worth was expanding in step, who cared? The lack of direct relationship between the reward to the manager and the results of the company bothered nobody. Since there was, of course, no direct link between the movement of share prices and the movement of the earnings-per-share figure, a perfect circle of nonsense was created—before the big letdown.

Many executives were caught with devalued paper fortunes; others altogether missed their chance to grab some easy wealth. As share prices descended, the value of stock options swiftly evaporated. The inhabitants of the executive suite promptly awarded themselves "stock appreciation rights." These allowed them to reap a rich harvest from any rise in the companies' shares while avoiding the inconvenience and risk of having to purchase the things.

What must have stung was that devaluation often occurred regardless of results. Many large American corporations went on raising reported profits throughout the Second Great Crash, but their shares suffered revisions scarcely less drastic than those of companies whose earnings were all but annihilated.

Yet no better engine than the option for the creation of personal fortunes is ever likely to be invented. That is one of the main arguments against the cult of earnings. The stock option gave managers a built-in personal incentive to boost the earnings-per-share figure. The stockholder of the sixties became the victim of the same process that had so smoothly defrauded his forefathers, when villainous robber barons forced up the price of their stock before off-loading it on the public.

In simpler days, the technique was to promise a dividend that the company could in no way pay. When it defaulted, the investors were left holding the bag. But this technique, even if it hadn't been outlawed, is little use in an age when tax considerations put share-holders off their dividend feed. When growth companies are eagerly sought after, the cash dividend plainly disappears from the equation. Some measure, yardstick or talisman has to take its place, and that something can only be the figure for earnings per share.

It is actually cut from the same cloth as something called the earnings yield, which is simply the reciprocal of the price-earnings ratio. That is, if earnings per share are 20 and the price of the stock is 100, the earnings yield is 20%, and the price-earnings ratio is 5: 5 times 20 equals 100—and that's the reciprocal relationship.

But the earnings yield, unlike the PE ratio, can be related directly to the dividend. Thus, if the above example is paying out 10 per share in dividend, you can say it has a 10% dividend yield, twice covered (which, of course, equals 20%). A twice-covered dividend is much more attractive than one with single cover, because it is that much more unlikely to be cut.

In this way, the earnings yield keeps in touch with the reality of dividend payments. But it isn't dynamic: quite the reverse. A red-hot stock, earning 20 a share and priced at 800, has an earnings yield of 2.5%, which sounds terribly small (as indeed it is). But that same stock has a price-earnings ratio of 40, which sounds fantastically high (it is). The ratio is simply a far more alluring method of stating the same mathematical fact —and without apparently relating to dividends at all.

As we know, shareholders believed that higher profits year by year would be translated more or less automatically into higher share prices. But the overall profits figure can't be readily expressed in terms that apply to the individual shareholder, in the same way as a dividend payment can, for example. Divide the net earnings between each share, however, and you derive a figure that looks much the same as a dividend payment, only the company doesn't actually have to pay over the money. Moreover, it's a figure with much more elasticity than a profits total.

The classic equation is that of the $10 million company, with a million shares in issue and a 20 times multiple, which buys another $10 million, million-share firm with only a 10 times multiple. The profits thus double, but the earnings per share of the first company will rise by a third. That might seem a poor exchange, until you consider the implications.

The two companies before merger had a million shares and $10 million of profits apiece. Putting them together, at first glance, can't improve the lot of the stockholders. The earnings available for distribution as dividend, or as anything else, haven't increased by a nickel. From this angle, conjuring up a one-third rise in earnings per share is worthy of any magician who ever sawed a woman in half.

The trick is worked by in effect withdrawing half a million shares from circulation and from the corporate sums. The highly valued company exchanges the above number of shares for twice as many of the underdog's. You could get the same effect by persuading a quarter of the top company's shareholders to tear up their stock and forget all about it. The amount of earnings won't change as a result, but the number of pieces of paper to which those profits are attached will be sharply reduced. Since the earnings-per-share figure is achieved by dividing net profits by the shares in issue, there must be a rise—and in this case a real one, since a quarter of the investors are no longer entitled to the loot.

But does the same truth apply in the merger case?

Suppose that both firms paid out $5 million in dividends, retaining the remainder for necessary investment. After the merger, the same investment is required: so $10 million is available to be distributed among 1.5 million shares, instead of among a couple of million as before. But it's not so simple. The investors in the taken-over company will have to accept a sharp drop in income if they go along with the above scheme.

They only have their half-million shares now, and their one-third share of $10 million, or $3.3 million, is $1.7 million less than they had before. They would seldom agree to a merger on those terms. But to match their previous payout, the combined company needs to pay $15 million in dividends—which means either investing $5 million less or borrowing the money from some other source, paying interest on the loan and earning lower profits as a result.

So the woman hasn't really been sawed in half. The realities must assert themselves sooner or later. The sharp improvement in the appearance of a company that has raised earnings per share by cutting the number of shares in the sum is like all conjurer's tricks. Once you know how the trick is worked, the mystery and the entertainment value disappear.

Not that the earnings-per-share figure is useless to the straight and good manager. Any arrangement that reduces the figure is suspect and needs to be carefully scrutinized to ensure that pigs are not being bought in pokes. But this control is essentially negative, a financial discipline applied to managerial plans and ambitions. It's a very different matter from making the enhancement of that figure the sum of all devices and desires.

The number of shares can be altered in several

ways other than mergers: the neatest trick is to repurchase the company's stock in the market for cash. Between 1968 and 1973, American corporations splashed out many millions on buying back their very own stock (thereby spending the equivalent of *half* of all the new funds raised by nonfinancial corporations). As shares staggered downward in the Second Great Crash, this stratagem had become increasingly attractive as a means of trying to stem the tide. But once again, no results in real terms followed the move. Even though the retired shares no longer ranked for dividends, or for allocations of earnings, and the directors had raised the magic figure without lifting a finger, that was scant consolation if you had bought the stock at a multiple of 20 and were nursing a fall of three-quarters in your capital. The boards concerned were making the best of an exceedingly bad job.

And many companies lacked the cash, even if they had the will, to use this device. As the market slump was followed by a genuine business recession, the squeeze on companies' cash flow intensified all over the world. Almost overnight, profit ceased to be the name of the game; the game's new name was cash. No firm ever went bust through earning insufficient profit, but nearly every bankruptcy is the result of a critical shortage of liquidity. It's a distinction that managements of large companies tended to forget until the recession of the 1970s brought it painfully to their notice.

Managements beforehand were pulled in two opposite directions: on one side, sound business principles tugged them toward minimizing profits and maximizing cash retentions. On the other end of the rope, the lure of the stock market (and of their own stock options) lugged them toward overstating profits and reducing cash retentions by the amount of additional tax which then had to be handed over to the government.

In America this beneficence was entirely optional in one unique respect. The Internal Revenue Service, while not generally given to generosity, allows U.S. companies to opt for FIFO or LIFO when accounting for inventory. We have seen that these heavenly twins, respectively first in, first out and last in, first out, have profoundly different effects which become more profound the more rapidly inflation advances. A company in love with FIFO assumes that the inventory used in making the latest product to leave its assembly lines consisted of the earliest purchases left in the warehouse. If the prices of its raw materials and components have risen since that earliest purchase, it follows that the resulting profit will be the highest which it could report (not *make*, mark you: merely report).

On the LIFO hand, if the company assumes that the latest purchases are the first consumed, the profit will be reduced by the amount of the higher price of the inventory. A company using 100 units of inventory in a year, starting with 100 purchased for a dollar each (=$100); buying 100 more for two dollars apiece during the year (=$200); and selling its output of 100 units for $300 can show a profit, after incurring other costs, of $100 or nothing, depending on which accounting method it uses.

Now, if a company has made $100 profit, you would expect to find the money somewhere about the house. But in the case above, the company has shelled out $300 in the year and only received $300 back. The sole improvement in its circumstances is that instead of

$100 of inventory, it now has $200. But the profit locked up within that $200 can't be realized until the inventory is sold as product—and, even then, only at a price a good deal higher than $3 apiece.

Actually, the situation is a good deal worse, because the $100 of supposed profit will attract corporation tax, which means that the firm has to find $50 of real cash (which it hasn't generated, remember) in order to keep the tax wolves from the door. All elementary stuff; yet, as we saw, it wasn't the simpletons of American business who fooled themselves with FIFO, but most of the larger corporations in America.

In earlier years all red-blooded American businessmen preferred to show the biggest possible profit to encourage the stock market; in recent circumstances, these same corporations have preferred conserving their cash to paying higher taxes. In many cases (following the usual procedure) managers were deceiving themselves as much as the shareholders. Like the latter, boards of directors thought that the illusory earnings which they were reporting truly existed.

The chairman of Arthur Andersen, one of the biggest international accountancy firms, put it as follows to *Business Week*: "The high-flying era of the 1960s was in many cases a misallocation of capital. It appeared to a public not fully informed that certain companies were growth opportunities. But then the sales started to slow up and you started to have other costs. It turned out that these weren't really economic profits at all."

Note the fine remoteness of the language. "It appeared to a public not fully informed" is one of those passive locutions that suggests that some personal force was responsible both for creating the appearance and

93

for the lack of full information. In fact, the responsibility for informing (or not informing) lay as much with the Western world's accountants as with anybody else.

Accounting conventions have so great a degree of elasticity that two sets of auditors operating on different assumptions could quite legitimately come up with utterly different sets of earnings from the same data on costs and sales—even the definition of a sale is a matter of opinion and disagreement. Thus the statement of total earnings could not be understood by the public unless it was also fully informed on the conventions that had been applied.

Now, if the earnings figure is elastic, and the total of shares in issue can also be manipulated, it follows that the arithmetical result of dividing the one by the other is a number of very low reliability. Certainly, you can't rely on that result to demonstrate that the real value of the business has increased, or that its ability to pay a higher dividend has been enhanced, or even that its financial future is secure. If the earnings per share plummet, true, that is a bad omen. But in many cases the augury comes too late: the oracle pronounces *after* the damage has been done.

Overstatement of earnings is concealed by rising sales. The company is borrowing from next year's profits, which can be maintained so long as the true earnings are advancing year by year. But when the true profits dip, the reported figures must bear the brunt of the earlier borrowings from profits as well as the losses from the present calamities.

This was the flimsy foundation on which the stock market boom of the sixties rested. The earnings-per-share figure is hypothetical: the ratio that links that number to the price of the stock in the market is evanescent; and yet managers, as we saw, fixed their targets in terms of percentage growth in that figure— as if by doing so they were fulfilling their duty to both the shareholders and themselves.

If earnings per share mean anything, it is as a measure of the company's ability to pay the cash dividends that shareholders prefer to shun. Yet the figure was used to measure nothing of the sort. To quote again from *Business Week*, this time from James W. Mc-Swiney, chairman of a conglomerate, Mead Corporation, "Financial accounting tends to emphasize reported earnings. The name of the game [there's that phrase again], however, is cash on hand and the future availability of cash."

Mead, in fact, could be taken as an example of the high-flying years: a sober and conservative paper company that embraced diversification and modern management ideas as its strategy for joining those few firms that would enter the New Jerusalem. Mead played the big-company game to the hilt. It even invented a system of matrixes, known as RONA (Return on Net Assets), to govern its crucial investment decisions.

And yet in 1974 the total return to Mead's investors, in dividends and the price movement of the shares, came to an annual decline over a decade of 1.01%. This ranked Mead at 304th among the 500 top companies listed by *Fortune*, from which you will see that around half of the above companies, even without allowing for inflation, had yielded a nil return to investors over a full decade.

Yet Mead, for one, had raised earnings per share

by a noble 12.4% compound over the same period. Not only was the pursuit of earnings-per-share growth by managers illusory, it is open to a worse condemnation still: to use McSwiney's phrase once more, it isn't even the name of their game—or yours.

10 What Goes Up Fastest Comes Down Farthest

Murderers may revisit the scene of the crime. Investors generally resist the temptation, and investment advisers find the resistance still easier, and still more necessary. If there is a dead body in the safe or deposit box or home filing cabinet, either it is given a hasty pauper's funeral, or left there to decompose, sometimes in the usually vain hope that it will rise again from the dead.

Only the rare intrepid soul seeks to recapture the mood and mental processes that led to the buying decision in the first place, even though the exercise is the best way of revealing the shoddy reasoning and the too easily accepted premises on which the myth of performance rests.

Ever since I started the practice in 1963, *The Observer* has published a Christmas list of the leading share winners of the year on the London market, together with descriptions of the men and the marvels that brought investors to the year's richest monetary rewards. The proceeds from $2000 invested equally in the ten winning companies listed in 1963 would have amounted to $6458 in the week after an exceptionally merry Christmas. From that fact alone, you know that 1963 was a bull year on the market.

That is the first lesson learned from a stroll down (or up) Memory Lane. New managements may wield new brooms, and old companies may dust off old stories; new stars may appear on the stock market horizon, and new meteors may flash across it. But overall the rewards and the kicks are dealt out by that impersonal, impervious and all-powerful entity, the economic cycle, with its sorcerer's apprentice, the long-term trend of the stock market.

No other study in the entire field of investment will yield you more benefit than the contemplation of such cycles. However, most people prefer to contemplate, not the skies, but the stars that shine, and investors are no exception. In 1963 the cycle had carried upward an interesting bunch of not especially heavenly bodies.

A number of the 1963 stars ended in the market morgue. That was the fate of the bearer of the leading torch in *The Observer* list: John Bloom of Rolls Razor, a skinny, skimpily bearded young man who sold washing machines door to door at cut rates, but coined a veritable mint from selling stock in his company to investors who fell over themselves to believe in the Bloom legend. Bloom also floated a firm called English and Overseas Investments, whose main asset was a holding in Rolls Razor, and whose main attraction was the unknown.

The paramount virtue of an unknown attraction in any stock market is that it defies quantification. So does an apparently concrete feature, like a historic growth rate in earnings per share. But there are some limits to the valuation you will place on a 15% compound annual growth rate. There might be some spiritualist misguided enough to pay 100 times the earnings, but not 200 times. The figure to be placed on English and Overseas, however, was a matter of whether the promised land would be reached, and how much milk and honey would flow.

The promise lay partly in the presumed relationship between Bloom and a much older, far wealthier entrepreneur, Sir Isaac Wolfson. The latter, with one of the country's biggest mail-order and retail groups in his back pocket, not to mention family investment interests worth much fine gold, had no visible reason to become involved—except for the small but profitable matter of financing installment purchases of Bloom's washing machines.

But the older man, whose love for deals was undiminished by the years, identified young John, so it was claimed, with the young Isaac of earlier decades. The enthusiasts drew an unflattering contrast between Bloom, bursting with energy and ideas, and Sir Isaac's reticent and industrious son Leonard, who minded the Wolfson stores.

Did anybody hear this story confirmed from any non-Bloom source? Had Sir Isaac himself ever told the tale? If so, those who heard have forever kept their peace. But it doesn't matter whether a market tale is true, so long as it is good enough to be true. That is one unfortunate reality of stock market swingers; they make such marvelous reading and telling. Bloom that year was an endless source of copy. Even his fiascoes were good copy—the home movie kits that didn't move, the bum Bulgarian holidays.

In a strange way, the flops strengthened rather than destroyed the uncritical adoration which Bloom received from the world. After all, it took a man of imagination and initiative to bombard the public with new offers, even hollow ones, and a man of courage to admit to his mistakes. And a man with imagination, initiative and courage—that was a man to back. No wonder Sir Isaac Wolfson supported him.

Or did he? Bloom's English and Overseas had soared by 800% in the year largely on hopes that Wolfson would take a major stake. Its big fascination was the unquantifiable bounty which would flow when the unconfirmed deal took place at an unspecified time in the indeterminate future. As history recalls, Sir Isaac stayed coy, Rolls Razor caved in under oppressive mismanagement, and English and Overseas only survived into a Bloomless future thanks to heroic work in the intensive-care unit.

Other dreams from my past swam out of that 1963 newspaper file. There were two brothers whose company, an agglomerate named Brayhead, promised much, duly contradicted by a savage and awful price collapse. The brethren then proceeded to try again at the tail end of the Second Great Bubble, with a far better tale, imaginatively speaking, than the first.

This last fable was a mélange of components for computers, exotic American connections and avuncular interest from Bernie Cornfeld's IOS. Cornfeld played much the same role as Wolfson in the Bloom saga, except that the less genuinely canny IOS got firmly stuck with shares of little worth when the second tale proved no more worth hearing than the first.

Another double-comeback was that of Klinger,

riding high in 1963 on an apparently irresistible tide of demand for machines for texturizing nylon yarns. In its previous disaster, in stockings, Klinger had been saved by these wonderful engineering designs. Its admirers the second time around did not know that Klinger was driving full speed into new disaster because of its interest in making the textured yarns themselves. Its impresario invented high production targets for the machines and set lofty sales targets to match; when the machines couldn't be sold to anybody else, he took them into his own factories, and there they proceeded to churn out far more textured yarns than the company could sell.

In this awful calamity, one story was that the inventory couldn't be properly counted for some time, because it was physically impossible to force a path into the warehouse. The can of yarns ended up in the unwilling arms of the biggest investor in the company, the great Imperial Chemical Industries.

Investors in the Klinger case didn't understand the fundamental economics of the business. Since there is some doubt whether the management did either, the shareholders can be forgiven on that score. But could they, or should they, have been able to uncover the management's uncertainty? More specifically, could investors have found out that textured yarns, not the marvelous machines, were the main force behind Klinger's booming fortunes? If they had done so, would it have made any difference?

No similar risks were taken by backers of Joe Hyman's textile group, Viyella; they might justifiably have shied at the obvious fact that Hyman was abnormally prone to publicity, and might also have worried over inevitable downside risks in an industry such as textiles, which is subject to its own abnormally severe cycles within the business cycle.

Viyella turned out to be the only substantial corporation in that 1963 bunch. However, nobody could have forecast that the recently forged connection with ICI, which had propelled Hyman swiftly upward, would have so strange a sequel. Hyman, the most creative manager in his industry, fell out first with ICI and then with his boardroom colleagues. They ousted him at night just after a celebratory cocktail party, at which the conspirators, like the assassins on the ides of March, circled around the doomed Caesar with sickly smiles on their faces. Eventually the company was thrown in with another ICI holding, whose troubles were only slightly less desperate than Klinger's. At that point the Viyella of 1963 finally ceased to be.

At least many investors of 1963 knew Viyella by its shirts, whereas few Klinger fans could have recognized a textured yarn or explained its uses. Still, few purchasers of equities have ever bothered to check their temptation against the realities of a company's products. In some cases, the wrong initial decision would have resulted; neither the first Ford car, the first Polaroid camera, the first Haloid Xerox copier or the first electronic computer would have created much confidence, but there's usually plenty of time, after the product has been perfected, to join the equity hit parade.

Often the billing fails to live up to the goods at any time. Bloom's washing machine range was genuinely inferior to those of Hoover, so his long-term ability to compete with the American subsidiary was deeply suspect.

What Goes Up Fastest Comes Down Farthest

A sadder story lay behind BM Group. This was the less risky alternative to Bloom's Rolls Razor vehicles and consequently showed a substantially smaller gain in the boom year of 1963—a mere 300%. By convoluted reasoning, which illustrates the essential irrationality of markets, the riskier situation often commands a premium over the more secure, which is surely the reverse of the logical relationship. BM's ace sold another washing machine door to door, the Imperial Automatic, several cuts above the Rolls Razor offering and aimed at a more affluent group of customers—moreover, the whole operation was masterminded by a computer.

Expensive door-to-door salesmen have to be supported by costly newspaper advertising; without coupons clipped from the ads the salesmen don't know which doorbells to ring. The Imperial answer was to gear the level of expenditure on advertising to the level of actual sales via the magic computer. The method worked excellently so long as sales rose or varied within reasonable limits. When sales slumped sharply (they always do when the supply of eager coupon clippers and door-to-door buyers runs down), the computer can't cope—except by closing down the business. Imperial ran into the same cycle of overselling and underearning that brought down Bloom.

There were much sounder businesses in *The Observer's* 1963 bundle, in sober lines of trade like sugar or gas cookers, building or upholstery fabrics. They were all second- and third-rankers, however, and none survived to become, as their backers hoped, tickets to the everlasting paradise. The list as a whole smacks in hindsight of greedy men being fed by a market hungry for bull-period profits; of reputations founded on nothing more than the movement of the share price (which then, of course, fed off the reputations that had been created by its own rise).

Another bygone of 1963, not on *The Observer* list because it was so small as to escape unnoticed, was an outfit called H. W. Phillips. Its capital gain in the year was even greater than Bloom's. Even perfunctory examination showed that it contained very little except some small interests making artificial fur, some allegedly miraculous but unrevealed processes for revolutionizing the textile industry and a fast-talking proprietor. His subsequent business demise left a number of first stunned, then outraged creditors looking foolishly after their lost money. Phillips was a British equivalent of the no-hope penny stocks which have never quite lost their allure even for the harder-headed American investor.

The moral goes deeper than the valuable instruction that bull markets bear to their top not only froth but scum, and that you must learn to look beneath the surface. In a few ways the excesses that this journey in the time machine back to 1963 revealed have been curbed since. But most of the horror stories of that era, a decade or more back, could be repeated with minor variations today—and are being. That is in itself a cautionary thought.

Another is that these blotches on the face of capitalism, these minor pustules, bear an ominous similarity to the legends of much greater companies, like Litton or Ling-Temco-Vought. The principal difference, as fantastic in retrospect as it should have seemed at the time, is that these operations, though founded, just like Bloom's, on good stories, rose to gigantic scale and genuine might. Even in 1974 Litton was the fifty-third largest corporation in the United States, L-T-V the twenty-ninth.

Those who backed them were no more likely to understand what Litton's management meant by "systems" than Klinger's backers were to grasp the mysteries of texturizing. If Litton's nontechnical top management spun a nontexturized yarn about their new technologies, many believed because they wished to believe. If people were informed that the "systems" approach explained Litton's past phenomenal growth, they not only accepted the tale, but also thought it entirely reasonable that "systems" management could be applied to make further fortunes even in a profitless business like shipbuilding.

Then, since James Ling was plainly a genius, even his mistakes (like Bloom's) had to be a mark of distinction. Like the Richards brothers of Brayhead, Ling on his far larger scale even managed to pull the same trick off twice: double-twice, in fact. His Omega-Alpha corporation was one of the last casualties of the Second Crash, falling to a collection of corporate vices which were identical to those that all but bankrupted L-T-V.

The master plan was to buy and refurbish dingy companies, which could then be resold to the public, thus generating proceeds which would be used to buy still more properties ripe for refurbishing. Just as Ling brought L-T-V close to its knees by his foolish foray into the American steel industry, so this time he gave Omega-Alpha a deadly karate chop by venturing into financial services. The operating losses on this buy forced O-A into huge write-offs and loaded it with $96.8 million of unserviceable debt.

Murderers not only visit the scene of their corporate

crimes, it seems; they repeat them. Both Litton and L-T-V, moreover, were sustained in their triumphant years by a touch of the unknown. Since the past in terms of the share price and sheer conglomerate growth had been literally so fabulous, what wonders could not be performed in the as-yet-unwritten future?

The principals of the two great star conglomerates also talked—and talked. Their candor was almost as engaging as their loquacity. No journalist ever left the maestro's side without good copy. No investment analyst ever went home to Wall Street from Dallas or Beverly Hills without feeling warmer inside.

They were not deceived in one respect: James Ling and Roy Ash and Tex Thornton, like the other heroes of the years before the crash, were clever men. But the three Americans and their corporations were not quite what they were seen, or cracked up, to be—and nobody was sufficiently interested in truth to explore behind the facade.

That in itself is no great offense. Explorations of this kind are difficult to pursue, however dedicated the seeker after truth. When *Fortune* looked into International Telephone & Telegraph, the supreme monument to the corporate empire building of the sixties, with its $11,154 million of sales, tenth largest in the United States in 1974, its assiduous scribes could find little to criticize or question, even in ITT's controversial ideas about accountancy. Yet the magazine, justly famed for its brilliant in-depth probes of murky situations, was visiting the company at the very time when, on top of the Chilean and Dita Beard scandals, ITT was about to run into crucial earnings setbacks at the Hartford insurance subsidiary which it had bribed the Republican party to keep.

What Goes Up Fastest Comes Down Farthest

The offense of the deceived investor doesn't lie in the failure to look for, still less to find, the truth. It lies in the fact that, even though the truth was neither sought nor found, investors chose to value Litton and L-T-V as if they not only knew the truth, but also knew the truth to be wondrous. All stock market meteors, with few exceptions, are made of the same base metal. The beginning and end of wisdom is to know that the meteors will fall from grace one day, probably sooner than you think, and to ensure that, whoever else is hurt in the crash, it won't be you.

You already possess all the defensive equipment you need—that most marvelous of machines, infinitely superior to any computer that will ever come from IBM, your brain. It needs only one basic input: the information that you are buying stocks solely for their investment performance, and not for anything else, from the genius of the chairman to the market prospects for textured yarns. Moreover, any fundamental data your computer does receive must be put briskly through the processing routine known as applied common sense.

Actually, you couldn't have a better model than the analysis that Samuel Mitchell—the same one we met as a lover of Xerox—uses in his book to explain why he never believed the stock market claims for the Levitz discount furniture business. Basically, Mitchell examined and rejected the Levitz case on the foundations of common sense applied to his general knowledge of business and what he could glean in particular about the furniture trade. Mitchell couldn't understand how, selling at cut prices, Levitz could make bigger profits than firms selling at the full amount on the ticket. It couldn't: which is why eventually the shares plunged from a peak of $60 to a low of $4.

If Mitchell had been as rational and fearless about Xerox's disastrous buy of Scientific Data Systems, he could have saved himself much pain. His in-built computer was plainly trying to warn him; that's why he suggested to the Xerox chief that "we" paid a helluva lot for SDS. But the "we" was his weakness. Past success and present pride had bound Mitchell personally to the Xerox cause. His own computer malfunctioned because with Xerox an emotional override interfered with its workings. Xerox, however much it grows and prospers in the future, is most unlikely ever again to be the stock that Mitchell knew, loved and called "we."

The only "we" in which you should be interested is yourself, your family and your bank balance. Keep your heart out of it—the next chapter should help you to use your head.

11 When You're Walking a Tightrope, Don't Sneeze

Most people never go near the stock markets. The silent majority deposits its reserves into the keeping of dull banks, dreary savings institutions, hidebound insurance firms and the like, where the rate of return ranges from less than nothing to a pittance.

The less-than-nothing return—which we earlier identified as "negative interest"—arises because the guardians of the people's money, at times of inflation, can't offer rates of interest that overtop the speed of decline in the value of money. But even at times of monetary stability (which have been few and far between), the small investor, who collectively makes by far the largest investments, is lucky to get away with much of a real, concrete return.

It follows that the smart guys, who know how to butter and honey their bread, sneer at savings banks and marvel at the penchant of the naïve West Germans for pouring their wealth into fixed interest deposits in good times and bad. Yet there have been years when the noninterest-bearing savings certificates known as dollar bills have been better investments than the supposedly fertile documents known as common stocks. Slumps in stock markets are frequently sharper than the double-digit inflation rates with which the Free World celebrated the midpoint of the seventies. Any smart investor heavily committed to equities in the off years is the true sucker.

The equity investor walks a tightrope, and it is easier to fall off than to get to the other side. The would-be Blondin begins from the point of necessity: he must do something with his money, even if it is only to wave it good-bye. If he chooses to leave his savings in cash or near cash (the latter having the advantage of paying interest), one decision has been taken, perhaps wisely, which is not to place the trembling foot on the rope.

The risk isn't simply that of the one off year. Over considerably longer periods of time, the laws of mathematics, which govern all markets, may make it extremely difficult to get to the other side. Take November 1972 as a convenient date. It was neither the best nor worst of times for the stock markets. Wall Street in the middle of that month had pierced the 1000 mark on the Dow Jones industrials, to general if uneasy rejoicing. The blows that were to strike London in the years just ahead didn't even figure in stockbrokers' nightmares.

At the end of 1972, anybody who had invested in the London market five years previously showed a gain of only 17.8% (coming down to 12½% after application of the local capital gains tax). Compare that with the situation of a nervous character who kept off the tightrope. The compound growth of an investment returning 5% annually would have been 27.6% free of income tax—and higher rates than 5% were available over most of the period.

At certain points in the five years, the record of an investor who came in at Year One would have been still worse, because the market had off years in Years Two and Three. Years Four and Five were better—they showed substantial rises of 21.3% and 13.4% respectively. But the glory of this performance was dimmed by a catch which I happened to spot: I wrote at the time that "it will take only a market setback of 18% in the next 24 months to drop the return of a *four-year* investor (who had the advantage of a lower starting point than a Year One entrant)" to the fixed interest level.

The cold breath of the Four Horsemen of the Apocalypse must have been hissing in my ear. The market collapsed to a quarter of its previous peak before the tragedy bottomed out at the very end of 1974. These harsh events are not needed to underline the point—that the magic of compound interest works in both directions. As con men down the ages have known to their benefit and the victim's cost, the mathematics by which 7% per annum over ten years adds up to an increase of nearly 100%, and not a measly 70%, is practically irresistible magic.

Even conscious compound-interest fans tend to appreciate the happy miracle of accelerating absolute growth more than its unhappy companion: the damage done by a break in the chain. Serious unhappiness will follow, for example, if the 7% curve is stopped dead— not reversed, just checked—for only a single year. If it resumes its 7% rise, you must wait not ten years for your money to double, but a dozen.

Investing in the market and sitting there has been

bad medicine for most of the postwar period, precisely because the fat years are followed by lean ones with such monotonous regularity and with such debilitating effects on compound growth. Here, the overinitiated will dismiss the whole concept of "the market" and point out, rightly enough, that this is something that nobody ever buys. Wise men pick selected shares which will grow faster—much faster—than the common herd.

But, again, we noted a flaw in this otherwise delightful theory before: selected shares, those in the superstar, high-valuation league, may also fall far more rapidly. Here, too, the knowing have a riposte. The object is not to select shares at their zenith. but to find a stock in its early, unnoticed days and to stay with it, not to the end of a rainbow, but at least to the penthouse floor.

The penthouse is indeed the limit for ground-floor entrants. But joining the elevator on the fiftieth floor or higher gets you a much shorter and less rewarding journey. Somebody, sometime, is going to book a ride at penthouse level, only to be sorely disappointed when he finds nowhere to go but down. And somebody who stayed on the elevator too long will feel a sinking sensation as the floors he passed on the way up meet him on the descent.

Ground-floor or low-down purchases are the order of the day—the problem is that there are so many ground floors from which to choose. The statistics of growth sagas like that of Xerox, né Haloid, read seductively in hindsight; but remember that Haloid was one, not in a thousand, but several thousands of runners. Statistics can also deceive; the magic of maths can produce the phenomenon of nonexistent supergrowth—something like Bigfoot, the manlike giant gorilla, who is alleged to inhabit the American West, who leaves vast footprints, but is never actually seen by any trained observer.

The statistics show, say, that a $100 investment has grown by 30% a year to reach a wonderful $1380 in ten years. But suppose that this investment has galloped up ninefold in Year One (by no means an exceptional feat for a well-lubricated stock in the take-off period), and then slows down to a fourfold trot in Year Two. The stock can then *decline* by 62% over the next eight years and *still* hit the 30% compound growth target for the whole decade. Yet on any criteria, for eight years out of ten, the stock was a total bust.

The number of such busts is legion, ranging from the big, bombed-out conglomerates all the way down to the Haloids that didn't make it. The statistical truth applies to earnings as well as returns. The ten-year growth in earnings per share looks wonderfully high for this or that leviathan of American industry and commerce. But a glance at the starting point of 20% compound growth usually shows how small the beginnings were; and a company that in five years quadruples its earnings (32% per annum), but then takes ten years to double again (7% a year), will *still* show a fifteen-year compound growth in earnings of 18%.

For a long time companies have ranked high in the *Fortune* ten-year-growth comparisons solely on the strength of early rises from a tiny base. The key is simply that a dollar stock that appreciates to $10 has done nothing special when it limps up further to $11; but that 10% gain, of course, is 100% of the original purchase price, and the proud possessor can now claim, perfectly correctly, that his capital has grown elevenfold instead of ten times.

The lesson hasn't been lost on the true, wised-up growth addict. Your best course after a year or two of supergrowth is not to hang on in perpetuity, but to seek another home for your superprofit. This unfortunately raises the formidable difficulty of persuading lightning to strike in the same place (your bank balance) twice. The plethora of investment opportunities produces acute problems of choice. How can you tell which Haloid is waiting to metamorphose into Xerox, or which of the numberless Nameless Corporations will stay that way?

The little company that will make it exceedingly big is rarely marked out by any distinguishing features. At the height of Wall Street's long, hot period, the keen young investor used hopefully to identify these animals just by the absence of the normal signs of credibility. If a company (preferably as far away from Wall Street as possible, in the Deep South or on the West Coast) operated in an expensive new area of technology, needed large, unspecified and nonexistent development funds, had a long string of losses and had so far failed to realize one of its many golden hopes, the fanciers would be overjoyed. I remember (he was wrong, of course) one of these explorers telling me, in just such a case, that "I've found my Xerox."

Like those who only back rank outsiders on the track, these Wall Street wanderers seldom did win. The game is no easier if the choice falls on a company that actually has a track record and is still full of running. Many exercises conducted by the shrewd have proved not only this point, but also the supreme shrewdness of keeping the neck well stuck in. In 1967, for example, a well-informed observer publicly named five entrepreneurs whose equities, it was hoped, would collectively multiply 200 times in twenty years.

The mind-boggling figure is another of those compound sleights of statistics. It translates into 30% a year, which I take to be the most that any mortal investor could hope to achieve over any significant span of time. After five years the Fearsome Five were all but bang on target—no mean achievement, even in that relatively lush period. But the individual year-by-year figures fill in with fact the fancy theoretical statistics rehearsed above.

The great bulk of the gain was made in only one year, when the five shares appreciated by 180%. Over the next four years, though the portfolio advanced against a falling trend in the market, the gain was so small, at 28.3%, that after capital gains tax it worked out below the going tax-free returns on an interest-bearing deposit. Once again, large gains made in early years, when a tiny equity capitalization met the full force of a powerful surge in earnings from a tiny base, saw an investment through many years of subsequent decline or stagnation.

Of the five entrepreneurial selections, only one achieved supergrowth in any later twelve-month period between 1968 and 1972. Supergrowth is defined for the purpose of this exercise as more than doubling the share price over four seasons. The best achievement of the other four was a 63.8% rise in one year by a financial conglomerate—and that was a recovery from a pronounced individual setback in the bear market, not a surge forward to new glory.

The conglomerate's comeback was in Year Four of the phantom portfolio, when the market rose by a fifth, and nearly all shares (by definition) rose with it. There is a compelling lesson from this experience about smaller growth stars: only the conglomerate at the start of the portfolio had a sizable market capitalization, and its value even then was a piddle in the international or even national leagues. The undersized rocket is a bad investment in declining markets, a good buy in bull markets—and there is some empirical evidence to suggest it leads heavy market setbacks.

A bear trend is usually at its strongest, scattering all before it, in the initial decline. It then settles on a Plateau of Stagnation (two stages better than the Valley of Despair which was explored in the First and Second Great Clashes). Stagnation is psychologically and financially an awful phase for a stale growth stock. If you invested for a fast ride, you get bored with a sluggish slide down, and jump off. Conversely, the market commonly picks up rapidly from the plateau, as do the battered rockets: only the latter fail to maintain momentum. (Those investors, would-be easy riders, who hung on through the stagnation are prime candidates for speedy departure once the pace picks up again.)

As for the Fearsome Five, none of them moved much after 1972, except in the wrong direction. A firm that specialized in finding holes in the ground and filling them with sludge disappeared into a larger group, and was thus preserved from any possibility of vanishing into a hole in the ground itself. But the purchaser's equity went into a swoon which cut the price by three-quarters, to the discomfiture of taken-over enthusiasts who stuck by the new shares.

Another member of the fivesome, a minor conglomerate, managed to decline in price in two years by over 80%. At the start of the portfolio the price had risen to an astounding level, 27 times higher than the eventual bottom of 1974, at which trough the equity had fallen about as far as a share can drop without passing into the happy hunting ground.

The bigger conglomerate hung on grimly by a series of liquidations of assets, barely surviving an almost equally cataclysmic fall: down to a grisly tenth of the 1972 peak in two years. Only the one solidly based industrial stock in the group, a chemical outfit, came through in reasonable shape. Its share price neared a third of the 1968 peak, but revived strongly with the market in 1975.

As a statistical curiosity, both conglomerate and chemical firm still showed delectable advances over a decade, thanks to that necromancy of early gains from small beginnings. But the hard-pressed survival of the one and the enduring qualities of the other left the high and ambitious portfolio hopes of 1967 in frightful shape—without even taking account of the fifth Fearsome Five entrant.

This was a modest-sized financial outfit which had grown by prodigious leaps out of an even smaller investment bank. The leaps were not especially easy to follow, since they veered from banking to insurance, from property to films—wherever, without apparent effort, vast and growing profits could be taken on board. True, the group did seem to wander into legal and quasi-legal controversy with equal ease. But that's sometimes a characteristic of companies that can't wait to move on at a cracking pace.

Old sages treasure (as you should) an adage even hoarier than their heads. Where newcomers are blazing ahead, and established firms—in this case the conservative investment banks—are trailing behind, the trailblazers must occupy uncharted and dangerous territory. In finance, the Establishment has the benefit of funds entrusted to its care since time immemorial. The outsiders must offer extra inducements to attract money, so they need to earn considerably more, when relending the booty, in order to cover the prime cost of their material. To earn considerably more, they must take far greater risks—as did our fifth entrant, which (for its pains, and its risks) has paid the ultimate price.

So what of the Famous Five, which were going to wax 200 times bigger in twenty years? After only eight years, two were no longer with us, one was on the brink, one was insignificant and only one had in any way lived up to its billing. Let that be two lessons for tightrope walkers who put their investment faith in balancing rods made of little growth stocks. First, one success in five is an excellent batting average. Second, don't sit on your first year of phenomenal capital gains if the stock or the market turns rancid—get out fast and switch to the investments that are most likely to resist a bear onslaught (if that's what is happening), or which have greater staying power, if optimism still rules the market.

We tightrope walkers, however, have a problem not known to the earliest investors—the capital gains tax. This fiendish device is difficult to cope with intellectually. We know in our heart of hearts than an unrealized 1000% gain carries within it a tax liability that is in no way lessened (except by inflation) if the winner holds on. But the gain, equally, is reduced by inflation, even if by nothing else.

The reluctance to sell, pay the tax and pocket the

residue has a minor financial aspect and a major psychological explanation. Financially, taking the profit and paying the tax appears to weaken your leverage: that much less money is working for you at compound interest. But this argument depends entirely on the stock continuing to grow. If it stagnates, then the untaxed residue placed in another investment will give you a better result, if it generates any gain at all. Those who pretend to hearken to the minor financial argument are really heeding the major psychological one.

The mind sees the original profit at its full value and forgets about the gains tax altogether. The switch investment, since it begins after tax has been paid, appears to start well behind the line in a competition with the original unsold purchases. But the comparison is misleading. If the switch investment doubles and the original stake, left alone, would have advanced to exactly the same point, it's true that the capital gains tax liability on the switch is higher. But so are the respective *profits:* by definition, the gross gain on the switch investment must be far higher than that on the unsold stake.

That's an outcome in theory, not in real life. And theory also notes that a new investment must outperform the old, untaxed stake by something like 1.4 to 1 to produce the same absolute net return. But if this fact is allowed to reinforce the investor's deep psychological attachment to his own successes, the equity tightrope can only lead from a rock to a very hard place—for the decision to let your capital gains run on is as likely as not to result in mediocre to miserable performance in subsequent years.

The simple antidote is to subtract the capital gains liability from all valuations, so that at least you are staring reality in the face and are psychologically ready for the pain of parting with some of the profit to the Revenue. That simple step is a giant stride toward showing the tightrope walker where he is going: which is the essence of successful investment.

12 There's No Safety in Numbers

Once upon a time there was a troubled investor. He saw in the papers what you will always find: that the rational policy is to hold a limited number of shares, probably no more than a dozen. This gentle soul wanted nothing from life except a little capital appreciation to provide extra money. But he owned forty-one assorted stocks and shares, a figure which is probably par for the course among amateur stock market fans (or professionals, for that matter). What puzzled this investor was that, by his own lights, he was reasonably successful: how could he be so right if he was so wrong?

He belonged to the Heads I Win, Tails I Don't Lose Too Much school of investment. When any particular share prospered mightily, his habit was to skim off the cream, and to reinvest the skimmed cream in another promising churn. If a share went to sleep, or began to die on him, he automatically sold, hoping to limit the loss to 15%.

This fate visited one purchase in four, an excellent

rate of striking in a world where, as Damon Runyon's Louie Liverlips once observed, all human life is six to five against. As for holding forty-one shares rather than twelve, this was another defense mechanism: the investor felt there was safety in numbers. Since one in four would go awry even in a smaller portfolio, the bigger number gave him thirty-odd potential winners, the smaller only eight.

Two things now troubled his former serenity: whether he would have done better, all the same, by restricting his purchases, and whether his practices had put too much money into his broker's large silk purse. Given the random behavior of shares in stock markets, the doubts were quite unanswerable, the kind of worrying question, like the identity of the Dark Lady of the Sonnets, that people carry to their graves. But the policy by which the investor lived in part simply rationalized a well-attested fact: the inexorable tendency for portfolios to grow, if not in value, at least in number.

Too few of us have the courage and self-discipline to obey a selling principle (like the 15% rule cherished above). We can always find a good excuse for clinging to a share, and some tempting tidbit is always around in the stock market (especially a rising market). So we retain the sleeping beauty and buy the tidbit, thereby increasing the number of holdings by one.

That is the virtue of imposing a limitation on size. It forces you to be truly selective, to ask whether the share at which you are shooting seductive glances is truly more desirable than the investment that must be sold to make room. In other words, restricting the portfolio is a valuable discipline—in the right hands.

However, investment is an undisciplined pastime. My troubled investor could have spared himself any anxiety. He was, after all, following a policy. If your investing methods work out, then you should by all means praise the Lord and continue to pass the ammunition. The only rational policy is the one that meets rationally selected objectives, regardless of theory.

However, it helps to venture along your chosen path with an eye, preferably both eyes, open to the pitfalls. The drawbacks to the Heads and Tails policy is so obvious that, as with large holes in the ground, many people fall right in. Suppose one investment blossoms like a flowering cherry, yielding a 410% gain. If the portfolio is equally split among forty-one stocks, the net result of this stroke of selective genius is a 10% rise overall. If the front-runner is only one of ten, however, the whole portfolio bounds forward by 41%.

That is the less attractive reverse side to safety in numbers. However, if one investment is a total write-off, the forty-one-strong portfolio comes into its own. It drops by some 2½%; the smaller portfolio suffers a 10% slump. The critical question is whether the chances of a spectacular success or a catastrophic failure are increased by raising the number of throws.

If you hold the academically respectable view that stock market investment is a game of pure chance, theoretically the odds must favor the larger portfolio. But that, alas, is only theory. Let us operate the Pin Test. A sharp pin stuck in a newspaper's list of share prices may or may not come up with a winner. But it doesn't follow that, if the first pin fails, a further twelve, or twenty-four, or twenty-nine pricks of the pin will do the trick.

If you enjoy testing theories, you can select random portfolios in retrospect. Find an old edition of a newspaper, prick in the pin, and compare the selections with the latest prices. A typical exercise of this kind, using my own pin, threw up one set of a dozen stocks with a 29% gain, only two of which were above the average performance of the set. But the soaring pair included one fellow that leaped ahead by 265% (as the result of a timely bid by Radio Corporation of America).

Another set of twelve pinpricked stocks included four above the average for the bunch, which this time came to 20%. Continue sticking pins in the paper for one hundred more random dozens and all you will get are similar random results. What else would you expect?

In any event, it's better if you bring thought rather than pins to bear. The difficulty lies in finding where reason lies in the market and how you recognize rationality. The Heads and Tails investor described above, who plainly accepted the rule of reason, had actually chosen an irrational course—and in one of the few areas where logic can be scrupulously applied. His success ratio (and his failure rate for that matter) should be precisely the same, no matter how few or how many the stocks he buys. He admits as much in describing his theory.

But if the same amount of money is divided among forty-one stocks instead of a dozen, the total in any one stock will be much less. While it is great fun and good for the morale to have a 100% gain on any investment, the pleasure is far greater if the profit is $2000 instead of $500. If your judgment is worth anything to you, it is worth backing with a reasonable amount of cash; putting less gold behind the judgment won't make it any better.

Moreover, if you insist on trying to persuade two-score stocks to hatch, as opposed to sitting on a dozen, you have so hard a task that, not surprisingly, you get driven toward some mechanistic device—like selling the whole investment if it fails to perform within some specified period, before the price decline has reached some cutoff point, like 15%.

The mechanism obscures an essential limitation which is even clearer in the Top of the Milk Technique, another popular alternative to thought—that is, turning any substantial paper profit into real money and letting the original stake ride. The stock market logician, confronted with some such plan, must observe that the investor is starting from the wrong point.

The place to begin is some overall target for performance. With that decided, you can deduce what individual gain over what time span will enable the target to be hit squarely. For example, assume that you want a 35% gain per annum after capital gains tax: that means an overall rise of 50% in twelve months, or about 4% clear of expenses on an individual investment held for a month (compounding can be ignored over such short time intervals).

Since half the investments made are likely to disappoint, and lose, say, half their value, the good eggs have to hatch out double. In other words, it makes no sense, from this angle, for you to sell for less than an 8% gain in a four-week period—net of all selling and buying costs. To be on the safe side (and safety is an essential part of the investment game), 10% is a more sensible target, which has the added advantage of offering easier arithmetic. However, it makes not a jot of sense to sell every investment automatically once it has passed the magic 10%—or any other bench mark.

The true question should be engraved on your wall: Are your chances of maintaining this rate of appreciation in this particular investment greater or lesser than in any other investment to which you might switch? If the answer is "greater," don't sell *any* of the holding. If "lesser," then what sense is there in selling only part, as in the Top of the Milk Technique? Dispose of the lot and seek that other, cosier home.

The question can be rephrased, possibly more helpfully. Ask each time you review your portfolio whether you would, at the *current* price of each of its contents, be prepared to put the *current* value of your holding into those shares. Thus the rational attitude. But investment, in addition to being undisciplined, is a most personal matter. The policy to be pursued must be one that fits your personality as well as your purse.

Most of us investors are torn between our emotions and our intellects, and this mild form of schizophrenia pervades all our decisions with a misty cloud of confusion. Mostly we end up seeking that contradiction in terms, maximum safety and the greatest conceivable capital gain: a combination which is rarely given.

The disease can be mitigated by fresh thought about the language in which objectives are formulated. That 10%-per-month figure, for instance, relates solely to the share price. Now, the basic axiom of stock markets is that share prices conform to no known law. In other words, the 10% objective is as rationalistic as aiming, when tossing a coin, to see it turn up heads. We can't escape from the uncomfortable truth that investment is a game of chance—but one whose hazard we can reduce to manageable terms.

First, a small digression is necessary. When company directors moan about the low standing of their shares, they don't mean its *actual* price in the market so much as its *relative* price. For example, when Philip Morris officers were bending the ear of the Los Angeles

Society of Financial Analysts back in 1973, they couldn't understand (with good reason, as later events were to prove) why their securities had a price-earnings ratio of 24, compared to 65 for fashionable, hotshot bets like McDonald's, let alone 99 for Polaroid.

Philip Morris was a resolutely unfashionable company in many respects. An American academic has written an article that purports to describe the amazing success of the U.S. tobacco majors in their efforts to diversify away from their medically insecure business. But the figures attached to this study proved that the most successful by far of the professor's three guinea pigs was Philip Morris, which had diversified by far the least.

While all the others had been busy minding everything else except the original shop, Philip Morris had set about doubling its market share of the domestic weed in eight years. There is something fundamentally unglamorous, however, about a business that puts in first place its basic priority, although that must be the business from which it derives most of its revenues and where it has its greatest strengths.

In any acquired or new endeavor, the management is forced to learn new tricks, and learning is an expensive process. Philip Morris was not above diversifying, with the usual concomitants of pain ("We have made rather sweeping management changes" at Miller Brewing was its 1973 version of the standard euphemism for firing practically everybody in sight). But hard graft in its own hard market explained the growth rating which Philip Morris didn't have.

Its aggrieved directors erred in concentrating on the misery of its relative price-earnings ratio. For the stock market is not concerned with relativities between A and B; the relativity that counts, as we have stressed before, is between C and D, the price now and the price then, when the investor comes to sell.

The same growth rate in earnings can translate (and always does) into wildly different share price movements. Nobody would ever have quarreled with the selection of IBM as a "growth company," for example. But given that the five-year growth rate for earnings back before the deluge, in 1973, was 14%, what would be the intelligent guess at the five-year share price gain? Would it be 200%? or 100%? Sorry—at that point IBM had appreciated by just 28% in the five years, barely preserving the real value of a purchaser's money (if that).

Polaroid's experience is even more instructive. Its multiple of 99 belied the fact that the shares had actually fallen by the odd percentage point over the five years. Since earnings per share had also declined (by 5%), Polaroid shareholders at that moment of equipoise had got off lightly. The figures had only begun to measure the consequences of the new camera, and the 99ers were about to see their faith rewarded with sackcloth and ashes.

McDonald's, on the other hand, had at least grown twice as fast as Philip Morris, at 37% per annum, and its shares had also risen twice as nourishingly, having boomed by 961%. (Which raises the interesting question of what on earth the Philip Morris management, after an astronomical rise of 431%, thought they were complaining about.)

That rough mathematical equivalence—double the earnings per share rise, double the share growth—shouldn't mislead you. For all these cases point unequivocally in a different direction. The growth that truly counts for you is not earnings per share, nor any other figure in the control of management: *the growth that counts most is that of the price-earnings ratio.*

That's the moral of our digression through the case of Philip Morris and its more favored contemporaries. The reason for IBM's disappointing gain is that its price-earnings multiple moved backward. If McDonald's had then dropped to the same multiple as IBM (which happened in due course), its share price gain would have almost halved. As the Philip Morris directors had noted, if their shares merely sold for the same multiple as Avon (only just, they thought, after performing better than the cosmetics company over the past five years), the tobacco firm's share price would have been two and a half times higher.

But there are always sound, or at least psychological, reasons why one price-earnings ratio should outsoar another. The future of any tobacco company is shadowed by cancer; its prospects, on any extrapolation, don't seem as sure as those of some drug company that might (for argument's sake) come up with a cancer cure one day. So the well-clad investor would not have reacted like the Philip Morris managers. It would have been as clear to him as the unwisdom of eating shellfish in Naples in August that tobacco firms would not turn into market pets this year, next year or ever. Which means that their price-earnings ratios, relative to the market, are unlikely to rise, and have a fair chance of falling.

Since earnings times the price-earnings multiple equals price, it follows that the key dynamic factor is missing—for the ratio is much more likely to be decisive than the earnings. In a marvelous year, earnings may double as the result of heroic, unexampled feats of management. But doubling of the price-earnings ratio (which has precisely the same effect) can take place in mundane circumstances when nothing in particular is going on—and so can a halving.

You as an objective investor should first inquire, when evaluating a share, whether the historic price-earnings ratio is likely to rise, stay level or drop (historic in the investment context, as we have seen, means any figures at all, since they all relate to the past, immediate or not). Only then is it worth taking a look at the earnings prospect—because only then can you evaluate what an earnings rise is worth in share price terms.

Bold theorists who learned no lessons during or after the Second Great Crash will object that there is a causal link between earnings performance and stock market rating. One year's decline in profit will sabotage a high multiple more effectively than an IRA bomb; three years of supercharged profits will do wonders to the shaggiest rating—other things being equal. The twice-bitten, thrice-shy can retort that other things never are equal—as witness the contradictory performances of the shares studied in this chapter. Many an investor has come ungummed through the false belief that splendid profits must lead to a prestigious share price.

A more intelligent way of sidling up to the issue is to question how the rating will perform given a steady earnings performance, and what would a steady performance be? To revert to McDonald's, the educated answer, as we saw, is that it sure as hell won't be an earnings increase of 37% per annum, doubling every two years. So you must postulate a considerably more modest growth figure—and with that done, you can see all too clearly that a multiple of 65 isn't going to be topped, at least for long, by that share in this world, and that a return to less exalted levels is as good a bet as this world has to offer.

A drop of one-third in the multiple, in fact, stood to cancel out a 50% gain in earnings per share, which, as I pointed out to anyone who would listen back in 1973, made McDonald's a far from juicy mince of sirloin. Time and again experience confirms theory, yet just as often investors ignore both. In particular they always tend to underestimate just how low high-flying stocks can dive.

The ideal investment—and some of these paragons have existed from time to time—would be a company with a good-to-stunning earnings growth and a modest, stable multiple. You would be certain that no nasty surprises were in store: as the earnings performed, so would the shares. Where these treasures can be found, however, is invariably where they cannot be easily discovered. The solution of that enigmatic sentence is that these are companies that the market for some reason or other has failed to notice. Once they are spotted, the alchemy of greed takes over: we start to prefer future earnings to present ones; the management begins to share the same illusion; and before the bell has even had time to toll, another fallen growth star is in the making.

Proof of this truth can be found in the very example considered in this chapter—Philip Morris. By October 1975, the management had far less reason to worry about its relative stature in stock markets. The share price had risen by 135.6% since 1970, compared to a 52% decline for the Avon whose rating the Morris men had once so envied. Over ten years, the 487.1% Morris gain stood against an 18.1% decline for Polaroid, another of the former envied.

The reason was that the Philip Morris multiple of 14 in 1975 had budged only one iota from 1970, when it was 13. In consequence, the full increase in earnings over the period had flowed through into the share price. Avon, in contrast, had suffered a catastrophic decline in the multiple from 48 to 19. As for Polaroid, the former 99er was now selling at 30; so, even on stable earnings, the camera company's shares must have fallen by two-thirds. Philip Morris had been saved, so to speak, by its Achilles' heel: the tobacco curse had averted the market's greedy attention from a 20% ten-year compound growth in earnings per share.

You can be greedy, too, but wisely greedy. Make your price-earnings assessment first, and don't buy unless you see an excellent chance, in the prevailing market context, of the multiple either keeping its level or rising. Set a limit for the multiple beyond which you are not interested. Ignore the seductions of those who argue that you should forget about the historic multiple (the one based on last year's reported earnings) and should instead concentrate on the current one (based on the projected or expected current year's rate). Shun this advice because you know that the historic figure already takes into account a view of the future. So when the multiple reaches your cutoff point, no matter how enticing the vista of the future, take your money and head, if not to the nearest tax-free erogenous zone, at least to the nearest bank.

When the Second Great Crash resounded around the world, far fewer smart money men were found jumping out of windows or perched on the sills than in the First Version. That's partly because they were less extended on credit, but it's also because some of the professionals had enough sense of self-preservation to follow the above advice, while encouraging less witty investors to chase the high price-earnings ratios into never-never land. Thus does money flow from weak hands to strong. It's no part of your role, however, to play Mickey Mouse to somebody else's Charles Atlas.

13 What Goes Down Has a Reason

Rain or shine, there's one question that anybody purporting to knowledge, genuine or otherwise, about finance and investment must expect to be asked first and foremost. The highest-octane investment banker in Wall Street and the little old lady with her all in AT&T or Shell both want to know: will the market go up or down?

Short of recourse to the Delphic report of the sage Bernard Baruch (who merely replied that the market would fluctuate), the expert is reduced to the usual run of two-handed commentary. On the one hand, markets will rise; on the other, they may fall. Thus neatly removed off the hook and replaced on the fence, the expert can go about his business, safe in the knowledge that nobody can hold his ignorance against him.

Why is it fair to describe the problem as non-exacting? Only because the man is being asked to predict in very general terms how a broad market will behave in response to certain known forces over a limited period of time. If he can't express a useful opinion on this score (to be fair to him, nobody can), then are his predictions on individual stocks likely to be much use? (As the reader knows, they aren't.)

Yet the questioners are on the right track. The most important factor in the movement of individual share prices is probably the general direction of the market. If you had a magic lamp, a greedy mind and one wish, there is no doubt what you as investor should rub for: an infallible knowledge of when the whole market will turn, and in which direction.

No more forceful and beautiful proof ever occurred than that shock boom in the stock market early in 1975. Although the skies were still thick with economic clouds, elementary financial economics could have revealed that the conditions existed for a sharp revival in equity buying. We've touched on them before, but they are worth burning into the brain—so you won't miss the turn next time.

First, a falling trend in interest rates. Rates that had belted upward in 1974 were now coming down. Second, the piling up of uninvested funds in the hands of the big institutions; these had gone on amassing insurance premiums and pension contributions undisturbed while the economic storms lashed down. Third, historically high dividend yields and abysmally low price-earnings ratios were available on many key stocks. Fourth, prices had gotten so low that there was little further to go— unless, that is, the world was coming to an end.

The rationale behind this fourth argument is that the index always has a floor, which must be somewhere above the value of the dividends being paid. (It can never sell at zero, unless all the constituent companies go bankrupt simultaneously. However, in 1974 some

London pessimists so far left their senses as to predicate a *minus* figure for their index, with shareholders actually paying others to take their property away. But this could only happen if liabilities were attached to owning shares, and that, thanks to the blessings of the limited liability company, is not so.)

However, this silly pessimism pointed in a sane direction: the cheaper shares got, the less people were likely to sell them. After all, if your possession is worth a large fat zilch, be it a stock certificate or a Guzzi motorscooter, you have no incentive to sell—so you won't. As the market sunk further toward the ocean floor, anybody not forced to sell by the previous price collapse was increasingly certain to stay on board. London saw an epidemic of "bed-and-breakfast" operations which emphasized the point.

Bed and breakfast is one of those eloquent British phrases, coined by some unknown genius, that passes into the language. It means that the holders of deadbeat investments, rather than cast the offending articles into outer darkness and face the losses like men, sell the shares, establish a tax loss, and promptly buy the selfsame offenders back. As the London market reached its nadir, many investors preferred bed and breakfast to outright sale. The implicit belief that their shares would one day show higher prices demonstrated a clear refusal to believe the world was indeed ending.

This refusal, since markets are moved by psychology, was itself an omen of much significance to those who were prepared to believe the oracle. Unfortunately, it's easier to follow the crowd, and it's a safe bet that very few investors, professional or amateur, got in at the bottom of the Second Great Crash.

When the first feeble buying of equities began, no

equivalent volume of selling occurred (because in-vestors, as noted, were still disinclined to off-load at subbargain-basement prices), so prices shot ahead. The crowds then rushed to buy before prices moved away from their clutching hands completely; thus the price sprint accelerated further.

The forces that influenced the market in the turn-around were the permanent factors that are the genuine, underlying makers of markets. To put first things first, we have observed before that the level of interest rates on fixed return stocks, such as government bonds, has a perverse but decisive effect on the level of equity prices. Movement holds the key to understanding; that is, if interest rates are moving in one direction, equity prices, sooner or later, must move in the other. It's the stock market's Law of Gravity: when one goes up, one goes down, and vice versa.

To which can be added the original Newtonian Law of Gravity itself: rates that go up must come down. And again the reverse applies.

Only those who are prone to look gift horses in the teeth neglect to buy equities once they become con-vinced that interest rates are going down. Unfor-tunately, both folly and overcaution are encouraged by refusal to accept that a ball thrown into the air must come down again. We congenitally feel that booms and slumps will go on forever, and only the brave among us have the conviction to advance against the temper of the times.

But the evidence is there for all to see. We broadly know when the market, or an individual share, is ex-pensive by past standards, and when it is cheap. We also know by definition that the market reaches its point of greatest expense, of supercostliness, just before boom turns to bust. So equally shares must be at their cheapest shortly before the tide turns, and money comes flooding back into a Sahara of desiccated stock prices.

Finally, the institutions have become more and more important in determining the volume of buying. It has become possible, within wide limits, to calculate how much uninvested money is available to enter the market—and the sum can be in the billions. The bigger this pile grows, the smaller the supply of stock on which it can be expended must become. That is because, if the big buyers are holding back, prices will decline. The 1974 gap between institutional buying and private selling was huge—small wonder that prices dropped so shatteringly. Sooner or later, however, institutional buying power (a) must come into collision with (b) investor unwillingness to sell at a loss. At that point, the accident becomes a happy one—prices will be raised by (a) until (b) gives way, and the only question left for the investor is when?

To know that the market must turn is easy: it always does. Calling the turn is a different, far harder matter, because it involves more psychology than economics. Any calm, cool and collected professional should be able to read the signs and give an accurate diagnosis and prognosis of the market's clinical condition. But nobody can tell exactly when or why the first fund manager will reach for his telephone and utter the incantation that starts the avalanche.

Ignorance goes still further. The professionals, the experts, the gurus are mostly none too sure whether the turn has actually come. Often they only discover that they have been luxuriating in a bull market, or agonizing in the throes of a bear phase, months after the event. Like weather forecasters who forecast a sunny day while hail is clattering on their windows, market pundits often warn of calamity while stocks are driving upward, and vice versa.

One expert I know, when the great 1975 recovery burst into flower, warned heavily that the bull market had not yet begun; a couple of weeks later he was proclaiming its definite arrival—just in time for the boom to expire in a temporary flurry of pessimism. This particular writer was a chartist, one of those seers who plot the movement of shares and markets on graph paper in the hope of discerning a pattern which, past experience tells them, foretells or establishes a trend.

For those who find charts too esoteric or farfetched, other omens loom large. Some New Yorkers swear by the movement of trading in odd lots, the theory being that small packages of stocks are favored by small investors, so a pickup in odd-lot demand means that the small man, like the first swallow, is signaling summer, while his departure means the opposite. Other elaborate theories are based on the relationship between trading volume and price movements. But any figuring extrapolated from market performance suffers from one plain defect: the fact that history is being asked to tell the future. This it can never do, even when the history is as recent as yesterday's trading.

This defect affects even my own favorite indicator, which is that the number of new highs and new lows recorded each day is an important guide to the market's temper and trend. This empirical observation, which demands checking by some researcher armed with files and computers, has much appeal. The idea is that a decisive move by the highs to outnumber the lows implies a cheerful change in markets, and, conversely, if the lows outnumber the highs, then no matter how strongly the market is rising, we are still firmly stuck in a bear trend.

There is a rationalization. In glooms it takes confident buying to push a share to a new peak; in times of affluence, determined selling is needed to force a share down. So a surplus of buyers or sellers at the extremes of the market, and against the market trend, may signal a wider and ultimately decisive change. But in reality my highs and lows say nothing about the future; again, they just describe things as they were yesterday—and what the searcher for signals urgently hunts is evidence of how things will be tomorrow (if not the day after).

One wise and good lady pundit I worked with subscribed to the engaging idea that investors-in-the-mass (by which she meant the market) always knew more than the individual investor. It followed that you should only buy shares that, on the evidence of low dividend yields, massive price-earnings ratios and peak prices, were favored by the buying masses. Only a good fairy saved her from total disaster, because the invariable truth is that the market chases its favorites up too far and reacts in savage, sometimes overdone fury when they disappoint.

The market has an uncanny instinct for truth in the opposite direction. If a company's share price plunges downward, despite the tips of the columnists and brokers, the protests of its chairman, the announcement of wondrous figures and bids—don't, however much you are tempted, dream of buying the stock. One time out of ten, you may miss a bonanza. The other nine times you will save your shirts.

What Goes Down Has a Reason

What applies to stocks applies to markets. The argument that there is no reason for the fall is akin to saying that your brakes should not have failed when your car plowed into a brick wall. They *did* fail; the market *is* falling, which means there *must* be a reason. The only problem for the disbelieving spectator is that he can't discern the explanation even after the event.

Identifying the cause beforehand requires less brain than nose, the same kind of educated sense that dogs and pigs in Perigord bring to unearthing black truffles from beneath the immortal oaks. I once found an infallible nose—the brilliant investment banker for whom a friend worked. Every so often this obsessed man would telephone his junior at home on a Sunday, full of desperate gloom about the market. This was invariably the signal for a full-blooded boom in prices, and I grew to rely on this somewhat backhanded tipping off. Alas, my Cassandra-in-reverse resigned in a huff one day, leaving me to fall back on mere facts in the unending battle to beat markets to the punch.

Basic economic analysis won't work as well as a nose, but economic data are the beginning of prosperity. The level and trend of interest rates; the relationship between stock market dividend yields and fixed interest returns; the proportion of savings going into the various investment possibilities; the relationship of price-earnings ratios and dividend yields to historic norms; the rate of growth in the money supply—all these are factors that must determine (and always have done) the bounds within which markets move. Markets move, moreover, in great sluggish cycles, interspersed with violent, short and sharp intervals, rather like a monumental gestation period.

The foundation for any intelligent investment program is an alert appreciation of the market's bearing and general direction, and a readiness to change that appreciation, equally intelligently, when the evidence shows that, once again, you've got it wrong.

14 He Who Crows First
Laughs Shortest

Professional is a much-abused word. In its simplest and most direct sense, it signifies anybody who does anything for a money reward, no matter how ineptly. However, the presumption is that nobody gets paid for his labors who isn't above a certain respectable level of competence (an unsafe bet in many fields, notably politics, bureaucracy and business management).

So the word professional, at its highest level, means a special order of excellence: the performer who knows to a fine point what he is doing, who understands precisely how to go about it, and who sets rigorous standards for himself. To such a model, the word unprofessional sums up everything that is sloppy.

That's why a Jack Nicklaus, after finishing high in a field of champion golfers, will head off to the practice course for three hours of hard work. That's why a chess grand master (like Bobby Fischer before his eccentricity turned to impossibility) undertakes a rigorous physical training routine for the world's most sedentary sport.

The pro leaves nothing to chance; unfitness might cause fatigue at a fateful moment.

Establishing how professionalism meshes into the stock market requires the analytical powers of a Fischer. First, since everybody playing in the market must be in the game for the money (although you wouldn't believe it from some of the deeds and the consequences), the pro differs only in that he spends most of his working hours at the game.

But the assumption that the pro investor—that's to say, the paid hand who invests other people's money in public or private portfolios—is a fellow who achieves a higher and more exacting standard of performance than the amateur is unsupported by factual evidence. The pro is often the first to follow a hot stock to perdition, to fall for the market's latest human marvel with all the *nous* of a World War I general stumbling onto the couch of Mata Hari.

Furthermore, it's formidably tough to judge the pro players in the market game. When a golfer consistently fails to qualify for big competitions, a tennis player gets eliminated in the first round of Wimbledon, or a batter never connects with the ball—then the dud results are plain to see and judge. But the results of most investment by most professionals are seldom seen.

If they handle private portfolios, only the private owners know whether the handling has been competent —and that presupposes an owner with standards of competence to apply. If the pros manage the great holdings of trust funds, only their boards of directors are in a position to make any judgment; since the boards share in the decisions and the responsibility for the decisions, they are in part sitting in judgment on themselves. So again, there's precious little evidence for us naked investors to judge by.

Yet if we are introduced at a cocktail party to a lean, bespectacled, well-tailored gentleman, and advised that the gentleman manages several millions of other people's money, we immediately feel in the presence of abnormal shrewdness, expertise, sense of timing and encyclopedic knowledge. We may very likely ask our new acquaintance for a hot tip—cr at least a hot view of the market, in hopes that some of the millions will brush off on us.

This illusion is based on the same phenomenon that Sigmund Freud saw in dreams: wish fulfillment. We want the world to contain infallible investment geniuses, modern Midases, for then we can hope to accumulate easy fortunes ourselves. Fiction encourages the fancy (which is, after all, fiction's job). Ludwig Bemelmans' wonderful tales of hotel life in the pre-Crash days of the twenties include a splendid piece about the perfect waiter who has spent years being tortured by a sadistic manager and ministering to a fastidious, germ-phobic Wall Street adviser to great fortunes. When the waiter discovers that his own market gambles have made him rich, he executes a worm's turn, insults and assaults the overbearing manager, and leaves the Hotel Splendide in retributive triumph. The manager, however, repairs to the market Merlin, whose wizardry rapidly reveals that the elderly waiter will find Nemesis waiting around the corner of Wall Street. Sure enough, the old boy is back, ruined, tail between the legs; he is humiliated, but then forgiven, because the wizard is unhappy with any other waiter.

The story is irresistible nonsense from beginning to

end. But it perfectly conveys the dominant image of the secret, powerful man of money, who invariably knows something you don't know, and who may, if you throw yourself on his favor, give you a glimpse of Aladdin's cave and all its treasures.

Any myth attached to human beings is bound to explode; in this the stock market doesn't differ from any other athletic pursuit. But athletic myths are based on visible signs of prowess. The stock market does include people with astounding memories and a preternatural gift for mental arithmetic. But while these faculties can be exceedingly helpful, like having a good eye for a ball, they are less valuable in these days of calculators and computers. Besides high intellect or numerical skill don't necessarily go hand in hand with high market profits.

The American market in particular includes many operators who have passed through business school. But nobody on Wall Street would attach much virtue to this qualification in itself; at least, not when compared to practical work. Probably any poll of marketmen would place experience far above any measurable natural aptitude or qualification.

Since stock exchanges are markets, and since all markets move according to their inner forces, the marketmen are probably right, in a limited sense. The truly experienced pro does acquire a fingertip knowledge from the experience of dealings, successes and failures, which can give him a sixth sense. He can develop the instincts that in pro tennis produce the percentage player: the man who knows which shot has the highest chance of paying off and which risks are not worth taking. In the stock market, however, those who listen most to the voice of their own experience tend to be overcanny; and many don't listen at all, but just tumble like any tyro into any hole in the road.

The mathematical marvel, the gnarled old hand, the newest *Wunderkind* and the most irrepressible gambler all agree on one thing, however: performance is the ultimate and only criterion, separating the men from the boys—but not unfortunately the pros from the pros. The full-time investment manager, adviser or broker can never lose his professional status, except by leaving the game. He remains a pro, a full-fledged member of the circuit in good standing, until he drops out, either of his own accord or at the instigation of receivers in bankruptcy and the like.

In judging themselves, moreover, the pros are as likely as the amateur to exploit their large lode of self-deception. We all like to believe that we have performed better than the facts are prepared to reveal. Most of us like to regard profits as positive, potentially to be taken, and losses as a temporary inconvenience, which will be righted and eliminated in time.

But the necessities of portfolio management force the pros to make comprehensive and accurate assessment of their invested values, to know to the last digit on their calculators how the latest assessment compares to the one before. Self-deception only takes over with the professionals when it comes to working out not how, but how *well* they have done.

The professional believes that all's well and has ended well if he has performed better than "the market," or, in other words, outperformed the index—even if he only means that his wretched fund dropped by *less* than the market. But if the market is down by half, I for one find it small consolation that the genius to whom I gave my money has reduced the values of my savings by only 40%.

I was interested in the example of Thomas J. Holt, a Park Avenue investment adviser who, according to *Business Week*, "has called every major market turn" since 1967—including such fine feats as predicting an 880 peak for the Dow Jones industrial average in "two to three months" from April 1975. It peaked bang on schedule on July 15—at 881.81. The extraordinary thing about this seer is that the hypothetical portfolio into which he places his tips hasn't set the Wall Street world on fire. A man who has called every major turn in violently fluctuating markets should have more to show for the turns than 173% in four years. The real impressive point is that Holt's hypotheticals did hit the 30% growth rate which is probably the ceiling for pro ambitions.

What I'm *not* impressed by is his beating the New York Stock Exchange composite index, which fell by 15% over the period. It's simply not a valid comparison: a selected portfolio, composed entirely of stocks that the tipster or the fund manager—both of them alleged experts—believes will rise, is being compared with a wholly random selection of industrial equities, which are meant to mirror the overall behavior of the market. What's more, the fund manager can put his invested money wholly or partly into cash whenever he chooses; he can switch investments, taking a winner at its peak, and buying a sleeper at its bottom. In contrast, the index is always fully invested in equities and never changes its composition—except when some stock (like the Penn Central or W. T. Grant in sad days gone past) disappears through a hole in the market.

So any professional who can't beat this competition,

regularly and by a noticeable degree, isn't worth much desk space. Of course, it's exceedingly difficult to climb when the market is sinking, especially if it's falling from heights of fantasy. But it's awfully easy to soar when everything is leaping upward—a fact which most pros are less eager to admit.

In sunny days, even if they did nothing but invest their patrons' money in the components of the Dow Jones or *Financial Times* indices, the pros would do fine. But since professionals tend to favor certain classes of stock, characterized by high earnings growth and lofty price-earnings ratios, which prosper disproportionately at certain stages of bull markets, they should quite naturally outsoar the index, without showing any cleverness at all.

The evidence is, however, that pros over the long run don't consistently outperform the Standard & Poor's 500 at all—not according to professors John H. Langbein and Richard A. Posner of the University of Chicago. They found that very few managed funds have achieved this trick—in 1974-75 the averages beat the pros handsomely. Hence the professors give their support to the "market fund" concept. Such a fund simply invests in the 500 constituents of Standard & Poor's in exactly the same proportions used in compiling the index, and never expects to sell a stock. This may be a good notion but it certainly sounds the death knell for any idea of professional expertise. After all, if every pro invests in the same shares in the same proportions, who needs them? And how can their abilities be compared?

Actually, relative performance is simply not a suitable standard for judging investment skill—including your own. True, the man whose fund achieves a higher return for its investors than all or most others must have something going for him—and who cares if it is more luck than judgment? On Wall Street, as the Crash was covertly gathering momentum, the leading trust managers were the gunslingers who took outrageous risks, placing large sums of money in stocks which had only tiny markets, with the inevitable result that the markets rose. But self-fulfilling prophecies are more manipulations than acts of measurable analytical intelligence.

Also, beware of the fiend or fund whose successes are won in a specialized market. Investment moves in waves from one market sector to another. In Wall Street in 1975, for instance, pollution control, truckers and coal were in favor; rails, finance and savings and loans were out. At other times, these positions might be reversed. It therefore follows that at some time any fund that specializes in a sector will come into its moment of glory, during which the managers can and do pat themselves on the back until their arms ache.

One group, for example, began life offering an investment solely in Australian stocks. Initially, as the fund languished, nobody had the faintest idea that new nickel wealth would before long transform Australia into the hottest pot in world financial poker. But when the heat struck, the fund's management inevitably seemed to be financial brains of the brightest order.

That is why who *does* best may not tell you anything about who actually *is* best. The good manager is he who consistently, taking one year with another, provides you with a return that preserves the value of your capital as a base, gives you at least the equivalent of a 3% compound annual return in noninflated money and tops you off with a substantial bonus in clear capital gain.

He Who Crows First Laughs Shortest

Nothing less than a satisfactory mathematical return at any time is grounds for praise, no matter how much the manager has clobbered the index of his choice, or how much he boasts about the clobbering—especially if the boasts are based on dubious valuations or unrealizable book worths.

Most pros never stray into such murky depths. They live comfortably off the fact that, so long as they score at all, the customers' bank notes will probably still roll in—largely because few of the clientele know what the real score is, or what constitutes a good or bad score card. London was inhabited until quite recently by trustees who had decimated substantial fortunes by leaving them largely invested in undated government bonds, a step about as wise, in the postwar condition of the British economy, as throwing a match into the tank of a car to see if you are out of gas. Yet the beneficiaries of the trusts didn't even notice that their fortunes were burning up until too late.

In making an honest assessment of performance, anyway, time rears its ugly head. Let us imagine that you have $1000 (or $100,000 or $10 million) invested on January 1 which is worth a quarter more on December 31. That isn't the end of the story, or of the calculation. How have you accounted for fresh sums of money injected into the portfolio and the market at different dates? Many naked investors don't account for it at all, because most don't want to face the sad truth that they are not such desperate magicians of the market after all. But in that respect, at least, they are no different from most of the pros.

Take the interesting case of William O'Neil, who every Monday sends 263 of the most prestigious institutions in America five pounds of logarithmic graphs charting seventy-five performance factors of ten-thousand-odd stocks. The 1000 weekly pages, which cost up to $48,000 a year, are almost certainly the most detailed research effort in the world, and *Business Week* quoted results in August 1975 which seemed to indicate that the O'Neil Datagraphs gave an excellent guide to purchases and sales.

But the same article named five stocks O'Neil said to buy, five to sell. On October 31 I had the unkind thought of checking on the results. Of the five buys, three had dropped by half or more, one was off by about a fifth and the other was down a few points. As for the five sells, one was marginally up; of the three I checked which were down, none had fallen by anything like the decline of O'Neil's three bad buys.

To quote O'Neil himself, "you can't kiss all the babies," but you should do better than miss their faces entirely. O'Neil claimed to *Business Week* that he had discovered an entirely new way to evaluate shares, based not on opinion, but on facts. The disproof of such puddings is in the eating. In the end, despite all the research, everything boils down to a subjective judgment —no better than yours or mine—of which way the shares are likely to move. Working away at the discernible facts of an industry or a firm may or may not have some bearing on this movement. There are professionals who study the movement of the shares rather than the characteristics of the company, and they, too, can be blindingly right—and shatteringly wrong.

These home truths apply to stockbrokers as well as portfolio managers, and they are well understood by an experienced hand in securities markets. Yet we naked investors persist in asking for recommendations of a "good" stockbroker—goodness presumably meaning the ability and willingness to put us, their clients, onto and into good things. But asking any more of a broker than to execute an order faithfully, and to pass on any information that has a bearing on our portfolio or investment plans, is like expecting the caddy to have the same playing skill as Nicklaus.

The stockbroker isn't anything like as interested in us, anyway, as in his fellow pros—he counts it a fine day when he gets a fund manager to follow a share tip. In that case the fund will place its buying order through the broker, who will pocket the commission; a handsome one, since funds seldom buy in small numbers. And if the tip proves successful, the broker can count on a steady flow of orders, possibly forevermore.

The courtship of those who buy and sell by those in the middle is a familiar racket. The lowest financial specimen is the insurance salesman, and the highest the banking go-between who brings borrowers of gigantic sums into contact with their possessors. But the brokers come well up the league. Any favor, from a blazing tip to a lukewarm case of Scotch, that can preserve the love of an investment fund is a passport to the good life.

Brokers need such passports, because their profession is singularly at the mercy of its market. Even if cocoa prices suffer a slump because some bug maliciously fails to destroy the crop on schedule, the actual quantities of cocoa consumed don't vary that enormously from year to year—and cocoa dealers will make a living. When stock market prices decline, however, the volume of trading falls catastrophically, too. The unhappy broker gets caught in a three-way squeeze.

Lower prices mean that commissions charged on a percentage basis become smaller in amount: Squeeze

One. The volume of trade on which commissions of any size can be charged is sharply down as well: Squeeze Two. The broker's own investments suffer along with everybody else's, and that is the final turn of the screw.

There are those who believe that brokers, with their noses pressed close to the market, always sense when to get out (or in), and so are sitting on the sidelines when their customers are being rubbed in the dirt. It is true that the members of the New York Stock Exchange have shown something suspiciously close to prescience by stepping up the sales of shares they don't possess just before market booms boil over. But this accumulation of so-called short selling at the peak almost certainly reflects not unequal wisdom about where the market is heading but the greater tendency of pros to speculate at all times; in the higher zones of bull markets, short selling is the most obvious speculation around.

Brokers are unlikely to possess foresight in any uncanny amounts. A professional who was truly expert at playing the market would need to be a masochist to drag himself daily into an overcrowded and arid district like Wall Street. He could just as easily sit out in Southampton, Long Island, enhancing his fortune with a few adroit telephone calls to the less brilliant brethren in the Big Apple. Experts, after all, have managed very nicely without shifting their base from places like Omaha, Nebraska, and that is a good deal farther from the action than Scarsdale.

Brokers are in much the same position as racehorse tipsters. If a tipster truly knew which horse was going to win, he would be insane to pass on the information to the world at large. The only result would be to raise the odds against himself, preventing him from getting any more bets down at the best price. The customer who asks a broker for a good stock to buy needs as generous a supply of innocent faith as the tipster's follower. He assumes that the broker not only knows more, but also that he is quixotically willing to share the knowledge for nothing—or for the relative peanuts of his commission.

The magic word, commission, holds the key. The tipster lives, not off the uncertain results of his tips, but off the certainty of his sales of tips. The broker goes one, if not a dozen, better. If he consistently lands his clients in the financial mud, commissions from the aggrieved sources will become scarcer. But very few citizens of the investing world follow their broker's suggestions exclusively. Normally their purchases and sales are an amalgam of tips from the broker, figments of their own imaginations, items dredged up from the media or the social round, crumbs from the rich man's table. By and large, the clients that a broker has, he holds—and not by virtue of the superior power of his advice.

The broker has a built-in incentive, which may or may not be resisted, to persuade you into the market. If you sit on your hands, or on a large pile of cash, the broker cannot earn a commission. His *raison d'être*, which is officially to help the customer deal, is in practice to make him do so.

The selling side of the securities business is uppermost, as it should be, since without selling there can be no profit. In good times, for instance, in the curtain-raising years before the Second Great Crash, the profit was abundant. John Thackray, a writer for *Management Today*, has calculated that for the 1971 outlay of only $300,000, a New York Stock Exchange member of strictly limited intelligence could plan on taking home $200,000 a year to Westchester. When the market slumped, the price of an NYSE seat slumped, too— until at the end-1975 level of $55,000, a twenty-one-year low, it must have been more of a bargain than any of the offerings on the exchange.

By the time the Crash's dust had settled, many fewer brokerage houses were competing for the business, the missing ones having crashed largely because of unbelievable commercial mismanagement. As business and share prices picked up in 1975, brokers could again be dreaming of $200,000 incomes, and thoughts could be turning once more to the yachts and other hallmarks of fame which had sometimes been forcibly sacrificed by past follies.

Any broker's advice *may* be good. Then, so may the mailman's. The odds strongly favor the broker, of course, if only because he moves in the world of markets and manipulation. Some of the rumors and rumblings reaching his ears could conceivably be based on profitable truth. Where there is smoke in the stock market, there is usually fire—the knack being to avoid getting burned by wandering, mothlike, too close to the flame. But most stock market denials have within them the seeds of their own contradiction. As a picker-up of these considerable trifles, the broker should lead the field. That still doesn't make him an intellectually strong analyst of the fundamental and superficial factors that will determine the movement of markets and individual shares.

The big brokerage firms, true, employ batteries of analysts to "research" into stocks and industries. Firepower like that of Merrill Lynch, preeminent giant of the industry, which used to spend $6 million on one hundred analysts, has tended to increase as a result of the 1975 change in commission payments on Wall Street. As a result of the switch to fully negotiated commissions, the big institutions apparently halved the number of brokers with whom they deal. The desire of the big brokerage houses to build up their institutional service has been met by the desire of researchers from independent companies to come in out of the cold.

The other factor was the 1975 uplift in prices and trading, for the number of boys in the industry's back rooms rises and falls with the tides of stock exchange business. In part, their employment is necessary window dressing to persuade the institutional clients that these houses have something to offer other than a glad handshake, a dry martini and a ready eye for a commission. The research work may be immensely detailed and full of nuggets. But the high hurdle comes on the bottom line, the dreaded place where the analyst must make his recommendation—Buy, Sell, Hold or (occasionally) Switch. And that is where he, and those of us who follow his piping, so often fall down—just like Jack and Jill.

15 Half the Heart Means Half the Profits

On the hard and brutal record of fact, you have no need to feel at either a practical or psychological disadvantage against the pros we have been studying. The pro's principal advantage is that he can make money out of securities by dealing on behalf of other people with their cash without showing any investment skills himself. If you make any money from the market, it's because your own money and mind have worked for that reward.

In itself, that's a greater advantage than might be supposed. It removes all extraneous factors. The pro, when jockeying to persuade his customers to take another crack at IBM, can't be interested in its investment merits alone. So long as they buy, he earns—and IBM is one of a long list of investments that nobody can be blamed for recommending (even though, from mid-1970 to mid-1975, the IBM advice would have cost you 18% of your capital). These blue-chip companies are unlikely to blow up, and whether or not you consider the buy a bad egg depends on that elastic quantity known as a time horizon: in other words, how long you are prepared to wait before the payoff.

If you make it too elastic, you will be throwing away an indispensable crutch: the knowledge that the uncertain future is worth less than the sure present— for two reasons. First, time is worth money, because your funds can usually be invested as an alternative in some medium that yields more than an allegedly blue-chip security. Second, even moderate inflation gnaws away at the true rewards year by year. If you buy with no clear target in terms of either time or gain, you are no wiser, no more sophisticated, than the French peasant who buries his gold coins in the ground.

It is easy for naked investors to fritter away their assets, since investment is generally on or beyond the fringe of our lives. Most people are mainly interested in their businesses or professions, from mining manganese to mastering the law of torts, and they are unlikely to give sustained thought and action to their savings. Even pastimes like golf, bridge, or transactional analysis get more attention, doubtless because they are not over-loaded with fears of risk and childhood inhibitions about handling money. But if you can lose your in-hibitions entirely, operate like an amateur but con-centrate like a pro, you may find yourself, relatively speaking, a superstar of finance.

The annals are full of worthies and unworthies who, having made a few honest dollars in some game or other, expanded them mightily by something often referred to as "judicious speculation." The list ranges from the supreme John Maynard Keynes, who knew his equities and currencies as well as his economics, to the heartwarming tale of the two Joes: P. Kennedy, father of the President, and Hirshhorn, the uranium king, both of whom supposedly sold out shortly before the fateful nose dive of 1929.

It's small consolation for the envious to set against those Joes the distressing experience of Cyrus Eaton, the only man extant in 1975 with personal experience of every panic in this century. He saw a fortune of $100 million sliced down, like salami, to $5 million in the First Great Crash. Not that $5 million in the valuable currency of the 1930s would fail to keep its owner warm during the long cold nights. As it happens, Hirshhorn's killing from getting out in good time was reputed to be $4 million—or rather less than poor Eaton's post-crash residue. The comparison only goes to show that stock market performance is relative, not absolute.

True, the two Joes began their careers as dealers in securities, which put them firmly on the professional side of the fence, where sat another mighty North American speculator, the Canadian Lord Beaverbrook. But all three used the markets as means to personal fortune and moved on to higher things as soon as higher sums beckoned. They were promoters, not mere sellers on commission, and their main promotions were themselves.

They exploited the opportunities afforded by possession of an inside track to create still more opportunities and still more money. They were entrepreneurs who happened to use the market in stocks as others did the market in wholesale groceries or carbonated soft drinks. The only lesson that you and I can absorb from their cases is to note the unwavering concentration on the objective, which is the accumulation of money, and their exploitation of the knowledge that a profit does not exist until it is taken: witness that crafty selling out in 1929.

Half the Heart Means Half the Profits

The amateurs who cause the most pain to other less successful investors (above all, to the genuine pros) are people like the British arc welder who speculated his way to half a million pounds in his retirement; or the American widow who, left with a large, young family to support, greatly magnified her husband's pittance by the same route. The stock markets, the investment columns, the investment banks, the newsletters are staffed with people who believe they know far more about investment than any arc welder or widow, dead or alive, but whose half-millions are nowhere to be found.

The widow and the welder had one asset, of course: time. Neither had the distraction of other work, and they could set about their amateur investing with that desirable combination of professional concentration and amateur assets. What have these amateurs got that the average or even the top professional hasn't?

In the first place, they have the virtue of ignorance. They may know little or nothing about "fundamentals," maybe not even what a fundamental is. Tell them that it takes in the extrapolation of the past year's earnings per share in light of the latest quarterly statement and the projected outlook for the economy and the industrial sector concerned, and these wise amateurs will still be none the wiser, and none the happier.

As for the technicalities, a point-and-figure chart leaves them (like most of us) as cold as the differential calculus. Advise them not to buy because a share has formed head and shoulders, talk to them about necklines and triangles, or some other gobbledygook, and they will simply have another cup of coffee. Even such basic concepts as the price-earnings ratio may strike little response in these bosoms.

Nothing confuses these investors in their devoted search for a share that appeals to their instincts—and there truly are people with an instinct, not for the market, but for a good investment—just as one collector of Spode consistently picks up the bargains that another misses.

It is a great error to suppose that these intuitive, innocent investors are really ignorant. Often, they are not only aware of their riches, they know the day's value of their holding down to the last penny—which is more than most private investors know about their portfolios.

Make it a basic rule to set aside a fixed time—once a week, once a month, even once a day, if you will—and devote that time to a thorough review of what investments you hold, whether you have more cash to invest, what you want to sell, what you want to replace and what, if your deliberations have positive results, you will consequently buy. The principles are set out in the next chapter, and most of us should never ignore them. Yes, there are amateurs who buy and sell only when inspiration visits them, like Archimedes sitting in his bath. But they have a touch of genius—and the naked investor can only legislate for the norm.

Beyond that rule, lines are difficult to draw. The problem is the same as that of advising budding authors. Each one must work out his own system of transferring thoughts into written words. But the investor, like the writer, needs to work out what kind of animal he is. It's no use spending hours polishing classical periods if your yen is for Mickey Spillane plots. And it produces nothing but grief to chase highly speculative shares if the past has produced plenty of evidence that in this respect you possess the suicidal instincts of the lemming.

Half the Heart Means Half the Profits

There are some investors whose instincts work in reverse, whose entire career in the stock market shows the sure judgment of the prewar German tycoons who thought they could control Adolf Hitler. In the first place, this class of purchaser is only attracted by outright speculations: so outright as to be far out. One medical investor (doctors, probably because of their scientific training, are prone to wild gambling on the stock market) had only to buy a stock for the company to go into liquidation. Once he even succeeded in messing up an accurate piece of inside information. The informed insider had advised him to place his shirt on Canadian Eagles. The doctor duly rang his broker and sat back to collect the profits. The shares soared according to plan, and with his money up, so he thought, by some hundreds of percentage points, the investor rang to sell. He was most put out when the broker commiserated with him over his *loss*. In his excitement, this surefire wrong investor had said *Mexican* Eagles.

His one rival in my experience is a foreign trade expert who bought shares of Britain's most spectacular flown-by-night, door-to-door selling company, Rolls Razor, *after* the receiver had been called in. Had he waited to pull the same caper in the same circumstances with Rolls-Royce, as not a few Wall Streeters did, my friend would have handsomely recouped his losses.

But the Rolls-Royce purchasers, apart from those with a sentimental streak, were gambling that the British Government wouldn't be able to shuck off all its obligations to the workers of Derby, the Lockheed Tristar builders over in Burbank, California, the Royal Air Force and so forth. Their successful gamble explains a great deal about the true nature of speculation.

To my Rolls Razor nut, speculation meant buying

something not only far out but dirt cheap. That is the most dangerous variety, akin to betting that the last ace will turn up just when your hand needs it. The word speculate (maybe already part-devalued by its close verbal relationship to "peculate") has been further debased by apocalyptic events, like currency crises and bank failures, which give the verb a smell of shadiness, of gnomelike intrigue, even of rank treachery.

But it only means wondering what will happen if some particular event occurs; the investment policy of the speculator is to act on the results of that wondering analysis. This is proper policy for all thinking investors. The act of investment is the logical consequence of studying the present, wondering what factors are likely to shape the future, and in what form. If you have no thoughts on the subject at all, you are reduced to random choice.

Pros actually go one worse: they look over each other's shoulders and try to safeguard themselves by copying each other's decisions. This breaks a cardinal investment principle: that the richest prices go to the hero who bucks the stream, not to the cowards who bob along together until they all reach the same stretch of white water.

The Rolls-Royce case was the simplest of speculations, which is why those of us who didn't jump on the running board should be thoroughly ashamed. Once it became clear that the government of Edward Heath was hamstrung by the obligations in the Rolls-Royce case, there was only one question to answer. How much money would the receiver recover for the shareholders?

With a valuable car company to be sold off, and with the government forced to buy the aero-engine business, the price was going to be far higher than a miserable few pence a share. The next question was how long before the payoff? It took years—but all along the route chances abounded for an easy cash-in. The old Joes would have pounced on this one like hawks.

Another case of classic simplicity was the U.S. dollar. I knew for over a decade before the Nixon devaluation that the old $35 an ounce price for gold couldn't be held indefinitely—not when a gusher of unwanted U.S. currency was spewing forth across the frontiers year by year. No profound knowledge of international economics was required. The business news day by day added to the certainty that one of those days would be the dollar's day of reckoning.

More than one old pro justified his label by seizing on this point as the only refuge from the dust and destruction of the Second Great Crash. One broker I know resolutely placed all his own cash, and the money of many clients, into gold-mining shares. He was simply backing a well-founded judgment of events, and deserved every penny of the fortune which he earned by such judicious speculation. (He spoiled it later on by continuing to extol gold and mines after the United States had begun to turn the dollar tide—the borderline between single-mindedness and monomania is dangerously thin.)

The judicious man, however, must do one injudicious thing. As we have stressed before, you must back your judgment to the hilt; half-measures, like each-way bets on horses, yield lower profits. Most private investors, emulating the I-would-I-dare-not hesitations of Macbeth, are halfhearted in every move they make with their money. They want to double it, but they also want to keep it intact. They feel that their choice is sound—otherwise they wouldn't be considering the purchase at all—yet they fear that some factor which they haven't considered will make their choice unwise. They either miss the boat entirely, by delaying the decision, or they underinvest in the situation.

Equity investment *is* a chancy activity. But there's no point in entering the lists unless you're prepared to take chances. If you are prepared to run those risks, then run them with a reasonably whole heart. Don't speculate with half your heart and/or half your mind. Think through decisions and indecisions. Remember that the main difference between professional speculators like the two old Joes and the common or garden amateur is not just that the former win much more money, and not merely that they are luckier: the professional gambler works at his game.

In that respect you will have to be as dedicated as Damon Runyon's late lamented Harry the Horse. Much can be learned about speculation from that unlikely encyclopedia. Although Runyon's Broadway characters preferred to bet on a fixed race (the *ne plus ultra* of speculation), they were not averse to a bet on an honest proposition. They were not concerned with the fundamentals—i.e., whether the past form indicated that the horse stood the best chance of winning—but with the niceness of the price.

In other words, if a horse at 2 to 1 was three times as likely to win as a rival gee at 8 to 1, they backed the latter animal. They knew that horses, like shares, are unreliable beasts (if not, why quote odds at all?); therefore the best gamble had to be the cheapest. By much the same reasoning, the tennis buff who thought Arthur Ashe had any chance at all of beating Jimmy Connors in the 1975 Wimbledon final must have fancied the 4 to 1 odds.

The above analyses all depend on some degree of lore. The best way for you to acquire that knowledge, that experience, that training, is to record, each time you review your portfolio, just why you took each decision. Then your reasons can be compared with the results: accurately measured, all expenses counted in and with total ruthlessness. That way you can get some idea of what works for you, what doesn't, which sources of advice have been most profitable, which disastrous, and what factors you have found it most useful to watch and follow. If you know what you have been doing in the past, there is, after all, a better chance that you will know what you are doing in the present.

On this foundation, you can build a more secure investment strategy than most professionals. You have only yourself to satisfy in the first place; second, timing (unless you need cash in a hurry) is a matter of total option; third, you can (and should) choose objectives that make personal sense. The pro on the other hand is often forced to chase after growth goals that are strictly unintelligent under the circumstances. For example, during the worse period of the Second Great Crash, even under double-digit inflation, cash was best. That's a justifiable choice for you as a private investor, but what possible rationale is there for paying a pro a commission or management fee to place your money in something you could perfectly well buy direct?

As with a regimen of exercise or diet, an investment course needs dedication and self-discipline; it's well worth trying. Take the $1000 test. Name the growth you would like the nest egg to achieve in six months' time. Then invest rationally on the first of the month, reviewing your investment each subsequent first. If you meet your objective, not only will you outdo most pros, but maybe there's a *third* old Joe in the making.

16 Inside Every Buy Is a Sale Screaming to Get Out

We have established, then, that to emerge from nakedness into full dress and prosperity, you should find out what kind of investor you are. In the end, you have only one investment adviser, yourself. Even if the secret and sage Felix Rohatyn of Lazard Frères whispers his latest intelligence into your ear, you are the one to decide whether to follow his advice, and to what financial extent. Even if you turned over your entire $33,756,-892.66 to Felix with full power of attorney, you, after all, signed the legal instrument. There is no escape from this responsibility.

What should you demand of your resident expert (yourself)? Are there any rules and regulations that you as dealer should apply to yourself as adviser (remember that if the advice goes wrong, you lose the money)? The rules vary somewhat from case to case, but there are certain semieternal verities, temptations always to be avoided.

For one, avoid buying any shares on the strength of other people's personality; that's a vice for journalists and stock analysts. The reporter is generally thought to be a cynical, hard-bitten character, with no wool that can be pulled over his eyes. But a man's judgment is always influenced by his profession, and the journalist's profession (like the psychoanalyst's) is to get stories. The man who has a good story to tell will endear himself to any reporter. But does it follow that the best story is the best investment? The answer is plainly no.

Financiers, whether they realize it or not, also know the value of a good yarn. One, now disgraced and reduced to cultivating his garden, was explicit on the subject. He described his problem to me at a time when everything was out of joint, including the price of his company's stock. As the wizard outlined the problem, the first story he had told portrayed him as a minor young industrialist who had developed a lucrative passion for equities while bedridden by illness.

The second story had him converting the equity passion into pelf by peddling advice to other investors. His third story was about how he built an industrial conglomerate (which happened to be the time of the ex-maestro's most lucrative gains). The fourth tale was the ex-maestro's conversion (much less successful, except in terms of sheer survival) of his conglomerate into a multimultimillionaire bank. Now, said the tycoon, came his toughest personal problem. What did he do for a fifth story? The only answer I could suggest was to tell the truth. Fate came up with a better reply, from the point of journalistic copy: the tycoon's decline and personal fall.

But whatever other answer had appeared, some journalist would have lapped it up. The satellite pets of the money world do swallow more than they should; they are too prone to flattery, maybe because of the contrast between their own fortunes and those of the moneyed men they meet. Besides, an unbelievably incompetent board of directors can put on an impressive show for a visiting fireman. It isn't hard, either, for an acquaintance to persuade you of his extreme ability—after all, you probably know little about the man himself, and still less about his business.

So never buy just because you like, respect or are impressed by the top magus or magi. Nobody outside a company has full or even partial knowledge of what the managing director's job entails. And nobody (not even, perhaps especially, a stockbroker's visiting researcher) can cross-examine the said executive to find out his fitness or unfitness for the job.

One expert financial journalist's personal assessment of the most exploded financial bomb in postwar Britain led him to call the offending company "a must for every portfolio." Every other writer has at some time or other fallen for a pretty talker. Another equally brilliant financial writer began a piece on another fallen idol with the remarkable and revealing words, "I love this man."

The personal judgment is irrelevant to you. You are not buying the man, but the equity; your sole concern is whether the price is going to rise within your time horizon. The quality of the man at the helm will, certainly, influence this prospect, but he may not be the decisive influence.

Edwin Land was as impressive when the SX-70 camera was savaging Polaroid's performance as when the first instant cameras created his and his shareholders' fortunes. The sole difference was that with the SX-70 Land had "over-extended the risk-reward ratio in a number of ways, ranging from the pressure on his manufacturing resources to the inadvisability of producing a high-budget item in a highly optional market at a time of cyclical economic downturn," to phrase the matter in the language researchers love. In other words, he took too many risks at once.

If somebody you know personally starts a new venture, or brings an established one to market, and you back him, the ball game is different. The ground floor is as sound a place to enter in investment as anything else. But it is this—the entry via the basement—that gives mileage to your judgment of the man. There is no comparison with the blind faith of investors who back someone they know only by reputation and newspaper or magazine stories.

One investor of inherited means, who as a top journalist should have known better, told me that he had divided his all between Shell and Mercury Securities, the parent of the S. G. Warburg merchant bank, on the grounds that Lord Godber, the Shell chairman, and Sir Siegmund Warburg, the chief conductor of the bank, could look after his family money better than he could personally. Closer investigation would have revealed that Lord Godber had long ceased to have any executive role with the oil group, and that the bank was well past the dynamic stage of its earnings growth (the period, note, when it was making its way in the world). A hungry fighter, as is well known, tends to win—and fight—more bouts.

All judgments made on personal grounds are subject to two acid tests. One, how much do you really know about the gold-creating ability of the alchemist in question? Two, if you were totally ignorant on the latter subject, could you still make out a convincing case for purchase of the shares?

These deceptively simple questions lead to another often broken rule: never buy on insufficiently considered impulse. Many investors base their buying on no better grounds than the hole that spare money is burning in their bank accounts, or the fact that the market has been galloping ahead strongly, and they feel like going along for the ride. Again, impulse may be an invaluable motivator for those whose intuition is in good working order. But it's always wise to ask yourself, when you feel the buying urge, whether in a less euphoric state you would have been at all interested in the investment.

Can you substitute an objective viewpoint for the subjective and come up with the same answer? It's a temptation to cook your own books—to tip the scales in the preferred direction. That is why psychologically astute decision-makers, caught on the horns of personal dilemmas, draw up lists of pros and cons. Not because they think they will produce an accurate balance sheet of the factors for and against, but because their subconscious will automatically tilt the outcome in the truly preferred direction.

So it helps to have underpinnings to your objective assessment. One is to search for some defensive factor that may put a floor under the price (the technical name, if it helps, is "limit the downside risk"). The possibilities include a heavy discount on asset value, a low price-earnings ratio, and a high dividend yield. None of the three is difficult to discover. The assets-per-share figure, like the multiple and yield numbers, can be found in any published data on the company—or in your broker's office. When the three are found in combination, you have a defensive share, which is not identical to a defensive position: risk still exists. In other words, just because a share price is overfilled with assets, rich in dividends and abounding in earnings cover, the job of selection is by no means complete.

You should then search for the explanation of the lowly rating of the equity. If the cause is likely to continue to create trouble, then the downside risk is unacceptable. If, on the other hand, the reason looks likely to disappear or diminish with time, the work is over; you possess your underpinning.

A second safeguard is that the company, at the price you are considering, should have a substantial market capitalization. If the market values the whole company for peanuts, it may not follow that it is good only for monkeys; but unless you wish to compose a wholly speculative portfolio of busted flushes, or recovery stocks which may never leave the sanatorium, shun those all-but-worthless offerings on principle.

Another way of investigating the status problem, and of underpinning the choice, is to assess whether the market price is based on some feasible degree of corporate performance, and isn't discounting miracles into the hereafter. The more the future has been discounted, the less that future can offer you in the here and now. This defensive rule is especially hard to obey, because it insistently rules out the front-runners in any bull market. So the fast-draw investor on the hunt for an exhilarating shoot-out will ignore the warning; on the other hand, if, as with most investors, your time horizon is years instead of months, you really have no excuse for walking out into a street full of flying lead.

The rule of investment is to find out which principles work best in your individual case, then stick to them—no matter what heart-rending profits are missed because the rules eliminate the wonder stock of the moment. Remember that for every long-term wonder performer, countless other stocks of roughly the same type become burnt-out cases and end-year tax loss candidates. Your rules and regulations need not forbid buying a wonder stock entirely; any worthwhile code-of-investment conduct must allow exceptions. But remember the rule again: unless you are a golden-fingered genius, those exceptions must be justified on some more material grounds than passing hunch.

In other words, our well-bred aversion to shares with high price-earnings multiples (based on the worsening of the ratio between downside risk and upside potential as the multiple climbs) needs to be leavened by the knowledge that in every list of a year's best market performers, some will have multiples of that very kind. If you are tempted, look for a sign of genuine and determined buying interest on the part of the big institutions, who are going to determine the price, anyway.

And you need rules for more than buying; after all, selling is an integral part of the act of purchase. Just as every fat man is supposed to carry within him a lean man screaming to get out, so every purchase holds within it an implied sale begging to be made. If you have no idea what that implied sale may be, you may not recognize the moment when it arrives. There are few agonies in the world of might-have-beens more galling than looking at the profit that got away.

Then there is the case of the profit that was taken too soon. Some argue that a profit can never be taken too early. And it is true that moaning about the 200% profit you missed by taking one of 100% is the same nonsense as groaning about the shares you could have bought and didn't. A beautiful old *New Yorker* cartoon shows a patient on a psychiatrist's couch reciting a list of lost opportunities—"I could have bought . . ." (In

175

1974-75 that same patient, very probably, would have been reciting "I *did* buy . . .")

The decision to sell and take a profit is a decision not to buy those same shares at the price you got by selling. The fact that you were already on board, but left the ship at your chosen destination, makes no difference—even if the argosy does sail on into uncharted and richer waters. You have to end every journey at some stage.

But the destination should not be fixed in automatic rigidity. You should have some general idea of the type of gain for which you are prepared to settle. The rule of thumb is that there is seldom any point in accepting less than double the going available net rate of interest, after capital gains tax.

Thus, if 9% after tax is available as a fixed interest return, you should be thinking of 18% net of all buying and selling expenses and capital gains tax—at an annual rate, naturally. After allowing for the inevitable full failures and semifailures, the net result probably won't vary much from the 4% clear profit on a portfolio in a month, or 50% in a year on a simple arithmetical basis, which we previously identified as a suitable objective.

The time-worn thesis, cut your losses and let your profits ride, does have the advantage of removing the necessity of decision, but at the price of sacrificing logic. Every time a share reaches the point where a sale could theoretically be worthwhile, ask honestly whether the precious object has any chance of repeating the gain. If the answer is no, or don't know, take your profit (not forgetting, again, to allow for all buying and selling expenses). If the answer is more hopeful, then prepare for a further ride to the profitable end of the line.

But questions about a potential disposal have to do

with loss as often as profit. On the law of averages, then, your problem will sometimes run on these sadly different lines: what to do when a share, far from recording a gain of 20%, or 30%, or 40%, has shown a like or worse fall. Don't let your ego prejudice the answer. Few of us readily admit that we were unbalanced or unintelligent enough to buy a share (or anything else) at 20% over the odds, so we decide that the share is bound to rise to the level at which we bought the thing.

It's true that in ordinary circumstances—not in the bizarre conditions created by the collapse of the seventies—whatever price a share has seen, it will generally see again, although the wait may take almost as long as that for Godot. *But hanging on to a loser on that excuse is tactically incoherent.* The business of investment is to maximize what can be managed with your money, not to leave the cash sitting there to prove yourself less of a sucker than, on that law of averages, you are bound to be.

Once in a while the market may have turned its back on a favored share in a fit of collective imbecility, which is when sitting on your loss will be proved right. But don't count on finding these Koh-i-noors. Don't join the born losers by arguing that, since so many thousands have already gurgled down the drain, it is tantamount to a bargain to send more money the same way. In investment, this kind of inverted logic becomes translated into the view that if the share was cheap at 100, and has fallen to 50, then the burnt offering must be still more of a bargain, and you should load up with many more.

The Charred Stock Theory has been dignified into a technique known as dollar averaging. As the share moves down (or up), the averager puts in an equal amount of currency, meaning that if you started off with $500, you put in $500 at each subsequent buy; so your average cost is never the highest nor the lowest price paid, but has a bias toward the latter. You buy more shares at the lower prices, fewer at the higher. The device saves you from the temptation of chasing a rising price too ferociously or crucifying yourself by clinging to an undiluted disaster. But dilution is the only good end that is achieved; neither by this mechanical device, nor by any other, can safety be plucked from danger.

Remember that self-deception is an inherent aberration in the psychology of investment. If you recognize this fact and learn to understand your own psychological profile, you will have a flying start. Unfortunately, self-analysis took Sigmund Freud several years; the process is unlikely to be faster for anybody else. However, the game of getting to know yourself in this field will be expensive—unless you are willing to draw heavily on your own personal casebook. And that means keeping an honest one.

17 Some Gurus Is Good Gurus

The fault with criticizing the follies of the men who brought down the Temple of Mammon in 1929, and of their sons and grandsons who all but demolished it in 1974, is that the criticism extends unfairly from the general to the particular. In 1929 and in 1974, the world of money contained many astute and impressive men, most of whose actions were as shrewd as their minds. In investment, as in other trades, there are geniuses and exceptional performers, noble whales amid the shoals of lesser fish. The trouble is that the stock market has the habit of seeing brilliance in every rising price. Which means that at times of boom, so many bubbles swell that the outsider has few means of guessing which is the hero which the future has-been.

The many long, distinguished and honorable careers made in the securities business have been founded on the attributes needed for success anywhere: work, application, honesty, the talent for picking and developing associates, ability to learn from experience and to pass it on, the power to distinguish good thinking from bad. The masters of the game would have made a mark anywhere, but happened to do so in markets.

Their distinguishing characteristic, however, is not electrifying brilliance and the sudden, Napoleonic coup. Rather, they are marked by their patience and modesty, and conservatism is their keynote. Ben Graham, the ace of security analysts, for instance, holds that the prime target of the investor must be to avoid actually *losing* money.

So these conservative gentry search out situations where the downside risk is small to nonexistent, no matter what happens to the market as a whole. This automatically rules out the euphemistically named "growth stock," those equities whose past record might encourage you to believe that their future earnings will support a present price far higher than you can justify on any present values. Never forget the two howling hypotheses contained in that definition: (1) that future trends can be deduced from past figures; (2) that the same value placed on the company's future *today* will always be applied *tomorrow*. Neither hypothesis is remotely tenable, which explains why growth stocks are as likely to grow backward as forward.

The good and true gurus are far more concerned with dividend yields and operating results than with market movements. So they seek out shares where, for one reason or another, earnings are undervalued, or where assets are vastly greater than their market valuation.

It's this undervaluation which gives you a base, an assurance that your money will still be there tomorrow morning. All true undervaluations get corrected, which is when the capital gains should flood in. Nor is it at all bizarre in highly taxed times to insist on dividend yield as a guide. A host of good implications flows from a high, well-covered yield: (1) the company's price-earnings ratio is low; (2) its cash position is excellent; (3) your capital is earning its keep in two ways, generating income as well as prospective gains; (4) since there are always upper limits to dividend yields, here is yet another insurance against a downward movement of the shares and of your nest egg.

Two classic instances of conservative brilliance quoted in Adam Smith's *Supermoney* concern the investments of Warren Buffett, a Graham disciple, in Disney and American Express, the latter in the wake of the Great Salad Oil scandal. The stock had halved as investors worried about claims for the nonexistent salad oil with which Tino de Angelis had worked one of the century's finest frauds; but Buffett found that in Omaha the banks were still selling Amex travelers checks copiously and that credit card holders were still using their Amex cards. So he bought and bought as the stock quintupled in five years. With Disney, Buffett saw in 1966 that the company was valued at only $80 million—no more than the price he placed on the great cartoons, from *Snow White* onward.

These are prize specimens in the menagerie of Nice Fat Anomalies, where most stunning stock market successes are to be found. The NFAs may be individual stocks, they may be whole sectors, they may be blindingly obvious, they may be discreetly hidden.

The gurus hunt anomalies with all manner of sporting equipment denied to you and me. Most of us can't, as the Buffett boys once did, actually take over a situation entirely to unlock the earnings which they were sure lurked within. Nevertheless, the anomaly can be found in many more easily penetrable thickets.

One example is the basically stable company whose shares fluctuate, often without rhyme or reason. A millionaire acquaintance of mine made steady pocket money for years out of a food chain that had an annual tidal rhythm. In the first wave the market thought it impossible for the rich, presiding Jewish families to produce yet another set of dreary results—on which idea the price shot up. It then sank down again as the families showed their perennial capacity to disappoint. Steady money in these situations requires steady nerves: taking profits when everyone else is hailing new peaks, and going back into the market a second, third or fourth time when the share has returned to the sludge.

With the tidal share, there is always the latent fear that the tide will start to flow in one direction only. But that's an unworthy inhibition, because the risk is quite small as market hazards go. The tides flow most profitably with big, stable companies, where bankruptcy or pronounced change of character are most unlikely. The signal to your alert mind sounds when a good heavyweight share of the fluctuating variety is flat on its back with a feeble price-earnings ratio.

If a company like Unilever, with splendid businesses ranging all the way from detergents in Germany and frozen peas in Britain to Good Humor ice cream in New York, sells at a single figure multiple, something is likely to be wrong, not with Unilever, but with the market. It happened in 1964, and the events of subsequent years are of absorbing interest to anomaly fanciers.

Three years of net profits around the $120 million mark followed, then four years in the $150-$170 million range, then a jump to over the $200 million mark in

1971. Earnings per share rose by 69% over the period —no cause for excitement here—yet the shares gyrated upward from their low in 1966 to a high in 1968 by over three times, after which they fell back by well over half in 1970, only to more than double again in 1972.

The price-earnings ratio oscillated in step, from under 10 to around twice as high. This skittish and erratic market behavior by a sedate and consistent industrial performer is manna from heaven to those in the financial wilderness. As a matter of academic fact, $1000 invested by a tax-exempt fund in Unilever at the 1966 low, and then sold at the high, with the process repeated every year, would have been worth $25,000 in six years, a performance worthy of the redoubtable Buffett, and one that couldn't have been bettered by many "growth" stocks in which the capital had been left untouched. By comparison, a straight investment in Unilever at the 1966 low, held until the 1972 peak and then sold, would have swollen the $1000 to $3000— not bad against the background of only a 69% rise in earnings per share, and further evidence of the defensive value of buying a cyclical stock at the point of anomaly.

But to exploit the anomaly to the full, frequent buying and selling are required. Granted, you can't expect to hit a precise high or low, even in a single year, and capital gains tax will erode some of the benefit from switching into the investment and out again; yet the point is clear—don't ever treat the Du Ponts and Unilevers of the market world as "lock-aways"—conservative holdings to keep forever as a base. A managed investment will normally perform better than one which is left lying, either fallow or fertile. It's poor policy to ignore the price pattern of shares, and it's the ultimate soundness, the essence of investment, to buy blue chips when they are cheap and to take the profit when they are dear.

Hunting the tidal anomaly demands the other half of the guru's formula—the patience that goes with modesty. You must wait for the moment to strike. With the tidal share, the moment comes when the price-earnings ratio is approaching its all-time high (sell) or low (buy). With the sleeping situation, the first necessity is to spot the out-of-line valuation. Then the assets and earnings have to be investigated as thoroughly as you can manage. If you are satisfied on both scores, you may need even more patience while you wait for your perception to be recognized by the market and by the share price.

Occasionally, true, the anomaly will turn into a far less charming beast, the Nasty Surprise. American Express could conceivably have been up to its ears and beyond in absent salad oil; the Disney brothers might have massacred themselves with Disneyworld or some other grandiose project. Research is intended to reduce this possibility, and the object of the research is to answer that single great question we posed before: Why is this share standing so low?

In the tidal cases, the answer is simply that the big buying institutions have become bored with the things, of which they hold millions, and in their sheeplike way have all been abstaining. Their teetotal action becomes self-fulfilling. Since nobody else in the market has much buying power to speak of, the shares in question decline, and some off-loading begins.

But when the institutions have somewhat reduced their lodes of General Foods, and the price has sunk to the bottom of the mine shaft, they look again. Their clouds of boredom lift, and they reopen their purses. The sheep dutifully flock in the same direction until the share is expensive once more, at which point the flock again no longer wishes to know. The action of the market tides is thus explained by something a good deal less celestial than the gravitational pull of the moon.

Once the anomaly is satisfactorily explained, you are on safer ground. Indeed, you are on fail-safe territory, where at the very worst you should, just as Ben Graham advises, avoid actually losing money.

There can be Upside Anomalies as well as Downside ones. That is, a share that for no apparent reason begins to move against its sector of the market until it stands at a substantial premium among the surrounding crowd. There are only two possibilities: (1) Somebody Knows Something You Don't; or (2) the market is wildly, ingloriously wrong. Either way, the case for jumping on the anomalous bandwagon isn't strong if you have weak nerves or poorly developed speculative instincts.

The only Upside Anomaly which invariably deserves to be hunted is one which arises from an undeclared offer for the firm's shares: bear in mind that many take-over approaches are vigorously denied before they are confirmed by events. For example, one of the most lucrative twists in the saga of Ford Motors concerned the large minority holding in its British company. In the eyes of the Ford moguls in Dearborn, the existence of this large local shareholding in an auto empire which they otherwise totally controlled was an obvious anomaly. As for outsiders, the more U.S. Ford denied the very idea of buying out the minority stake at a fat profit for the holders, the more logical it seemed.

The brighter investors realized to their future profit

that when an international firm, especially an American one, buys a local outfit, it always pays over the odds, partly as an insurance against political opposition.

The bias of the courts and others in favor of minority shareholders also helps. An anomalous portfolio of minority holdings in firms controlled by larger companies can meet the fail-safe considerations in every respect, especially if the rumors of rich rationalization have already started to circulate.

But mere mention of take-over possibilities is not enough—not at all the same thing as a nice, meaty Wall Street rumor, well-dusted in bread crumbs and denied to a turn. Whether these whispers actually start from genuine information, derived from the chauffeur's mouth, is irrelevant, given their high accuracy ratio over the years. Nor is everything lost if you have ignored or not heard the rumor. The offer may be contested. In that case, there is usually more to go for. I have often sat there swearing at my missed opportunity each time some bauble being fought over in the market has risen by another 20%.

Again, there are only two possibilities. Either the defense will succeed, which can only mean persuading holders that the shares are worth more than the bid price. Or the defense will fail, in which case the shares will be bought for at least the current price. That's fail-safe spiced with a pinch of adventure: the best of all possible worlds.

The anomalous element in contested bids for a company's stock lies in the fact that the bidder is willing to pay above the market price, possibly because of an underlying business anomaly, possibly because the bidder is set on a flight of fantasy. But as 1975 came to its end, more and more evidence accumulated to show that the most humdrum of all anomalies repay hunting —those being my beloved companies that, while perfectly sound of wind and limb, offer high dividend yields.

On both sides of the Atlantic, "defensive" funds, specializing in the above kinds of stock, have done so much better than aggressive ones that it will take years for the latter to catch up. In 1973-75, which included two horror years, the income funds, according to Computer Directions Advisors, were up 4%. "Aggressive growth" funds were down 33%. In 1975—a bull year— the aggressors led the defenders by 33% to 28%. At the latter rates, do you know how long it would take for the faster-moving offensive team to catch up on our favorites? Don't waste your time working it out—it's every bit of *thirteen years*.

The Defensive Anomaly arises from the market's perversity in paying more for less when it fixes a *higher* price on the security offering a *lower* return. It is in these lists that the anomaly hunter can find his fail-safe reward. If you fail to find an anomaly that will be corrected, your high dividend yield should leave you relatively safe. If the correction does take place, your hunting has in practice achieved the theoretically impossible: that perfect combination of high yield and abundant capital gain.

18 If the Price Is Right, Take It

Throughout the sixties, equity values were kept buoyant in part by the insatiable appetite of corporations for each other. The big boys, except for the conglomerate rampagers, were mostly kept out of this feast by political or legal pressures; but among private companies, public firms, family-controlled enterprises, widely held corporations, small outfits, big brothers, the enthusiasm for corporate purchase swept them all. Even in the United States, for all its antitrust activities, the merger wave rushed on lower down, while the big actions, against the likes of ITT and IBM, rumbled on in the upper regions.

Was the Second Crash partly caused by the peaking out of the amalgamation boom? The take-over by exchange of shares brought an element of phoniness into markets, like watering the stock in more innocently crooked days. The amalgamation merchants issued great gouts of securities, far more than the market would have absorbed in any other circumstances, in exchange for the paper of the desired company. It was an apparently painless method of issuing shares without actually having to test the willingness of the market to pay their going price. And it had the far from incidental benefit of adding earnings and prestige to the purchasers.

The fever for these "acquisition strategies" died from a cause that reversed the reasoning that originally promoted the intensity: the stock market boom faded. Those who believe that higher reason must govern markets should wonder why the pitch of amalgamation activity always rises when stock prices are at their zenith. Surely the wise corporation, like the wise investor, would buy companies when they were cheap, not the other way around—even if the buys were only cheap in terms of its own stock. Yet, we have seen that the smartest and slickest gentry around (at least in their own estimation) habitually paid prices that were expensive in relation to their own stock.

The paradox can be explained both by psychology and by monetary economics. First, the share boom is contagious, and managements get sucked into the action, and into the desire to contribute to that action. Second, at the same time, all market booms are fed by easy money. Firms as well as personal bank accounts are awash in the monetary flood, and the joy in acquisition is financially unconfined.

In market depressions, the engine goes into reverse. The psychology of managements is darkened both by the contagion of financial woes and by the worsening of business conditions which goes with the market fall. Those conditions almost certainly include a clampdown on the money supply and rising interest rates. When the business cycle has rotated still further, and credit is easy once more, corporate managements, licking their wounds, begin to move into merger action only slowly, until general confidence returns both to the stock market and the economy.

In the last chapter, we noted that the uninvolved investor can hope to take a free ride on the merger swings and roundabouts. But what about the investor who is already on board, either with the attacking pirate or on the galleon loaded with gold? Attitudes tend to vary sharply depending on which side the person striking the attitude happens to stand. Otis Elevator, threatened by a marauding United Technologies, reacted in 1975 in the time-honored offended style: an affront which could only be assuaged by more money—and that's all that should ever count.

The essence of a property-owning democracy is that what's owned can be disowned; what's bought, sold; what's offered, accepted. If the job of directors is to maximize the shareholders' wealth, and the job of the shareholders is to pocket the proceeds wherever they find them, then they and you must forget loyalty, patriotism, idealism and everything else. If the price *is* right, you must be right to take it.

The matter of mergers is by no means as one-sided as liberal economists believe. True, the public interest is defined by preserving small- to medium-scale enterprise and by preventing the weighty from getting too big for our boots. But the public interest is also defended by keeping a sword of Damocles hanging over the heads of boards of directors, a sword that will drop if their record fails to satisfy the stockholders.

Better still, when a board has failed for long years, an offer for the shares may accomplish as much good for the shareholders overnight as decades of dynamic expansion. There's simply no substitute for an over-generous bid when it comes to lining bare pockets.

If the Price Is Right, Take It

In 1974, when Rockwell International bought Admiral Corporation, it was one of the few conglomerates still buying. The purchase—Rockwell's twenty-third in eight years—came just in time to save Admiral shareholders from bearing huge losses: $15-$20 million in the first full fiscal year under Rockwell, whose president put the matter in a nutshell to *Business Week*. If they had foreseen what was going to happen to the economy, "we would have delayed the purchase and got them at a lot better price." But Rockwell's loss was Admiral's gain. The moral is plain: no bids are bad news for investors at the *receiving* end.

But the strong probability is that future markets will lack the old artificial merger stimulus, at least to the degree of the sixties. Directors have become more adroit at resisting boarders (like the American company which, faced with unwanted advances from Litton Industries, which had a furniture subsidiary, promptly bought a couple of furniture companies itself, so as to produce an antimonopoly defense). The rules of the authorities have also become increasingly inhibiting. Individual shareholders, too, mostly remain sunk in an everlasting, loyal apathy. And the big institutions as shareholders still perenially sit on the fence, getting off only to join the side of the Establishment.

Many of the former big spenders, furthermore, must have lost their lust for corporate girls of easy virtue. Rockwell's twenty-three-merger binge helped to push up its debt to over a billion, while cash was draining out of the company at $30 million a month. Small wonder that Rockwell tried—unsuccessfully, as it turned out—to part Gulf Oil from $200 million in exchange for a fifth of the company: if your own buys beat you, seek a buyer yourself. At the very least, you won't buy again in a hurry.

Although the merger mania contributed mightily to the boom of the sixties in the short term, in the long run the amalgamations undermined the strength of the market. The purchaser who paid too much for the victim, thus weakening the combined equity's underlying base of profits, simultaneously proceeded, as we have seen, to weaken the stock by creating considerably more of his paper than ever existed before. In this drastically altered supply-demand relationship, only the most extraordinary feats, or incredible faith, can keep up the share price. And the feats are most unlikely to come about from a friendly deal. It's the hostile attack that may pay off—a management that comes out on top in a corporate wrestling match at least gains carte blanche to tear away at the acquired body. And dissection and resection are generally the only ways in which to extract benefit for the shareholders.

But judgment on the consequences of mergers is a matter of difficult balance, like that on Victorian painting, in which the good and great is frequently offset by the awful and trite. The best guide, as always, is the best interest of you, the individual shareholder. The purpose of your holding an investment is to reach the day when somebody else will pay more for it than it cost. The removal of cash-rich predators eliminates a potential purchasing force, and is thus a great pity, at least from this narrow viewpoint.

There is only one test: which alternative (accept or reject) will produce the largest amount of cash in hand? That amount is verifiable fact; anything else is pure speculation about an impure (i.e., uncertain) future. The cash test applies whether your company is being bought or buying. If a price is wrong, as you well know, a deal cannot be right. After all, if you are offered shares—any shares—at a quarter above the going market price, you won't exactly jump at the bargain.

All considerations of the national economic weal should be totally beside the point for you. Ignore the amazing views of one professor who believes that ". . . the merger is part of the process by which efficient firms grow . . . it may be regarded as a civilized alternative to the bankruptcy of the unsuccessful firms." Not only is there no guarantee that the company that grows by merger is efficient, but take-overs of this variety are in the minority. Most mergers are consummated between firms of roughly equal competence, one of which simply happens to be larger.

Another learned academic holds that "assets are typically more effectively operated after they have been removed from their acquisition management. Much of the evidence for this contention comes from the United States . . ." Does it? The Federal Trade Commission spent three years studying nine conglomerates and found no significant differences in the management or the performance of the 348 companies devoured by these corporate wolves in the period 1960-68. In theory some of these purchases were ideal demonstrations of the beneficial effects of mergers—when a big company buys into a concentrated industry by taking on one of the smaller units, and blending its own muscle with the smaller unit's market experience. More often than not, according to the FTC, the acquired company wound up with a *smaller* share of its markets than before the take-over geniuses moved in.

In actuality, figures are so rarely published to show how well or ill the taken-over outfit has performed under its new aegis that no defender of the merger faith can have much of a statistical leg to stand on. The new subsidiary simply gets lost in the maze of corporate accounting.

When one devoted mergergrubber of the bull years sprang to his own defense a few years before his financial demise, the facts of his largest acquisition were paraded as conclusive evidence. When he finally sold off the jewel, the purchasers' accountants came to the early, miffed conclusion that the profits—on which the claims of conglomerate management excellence were based—had been overstated by about half. Of such large and small self-deceits were the conglomerate stories partly made, and those deceived were often to be found among the pros in the investment community.

Prose poems about the working methods of any acquisitive management are nothing but *post hoc* rationalizations of ways of managing which work well as long as they work well, which means until (inevitably) they fail. The company executive who buys another company, anyway, is not actually managing at the moment of purchase, but investing. He is in exactly the same position as you and I when we invest, except that (1) he usually has to buy all the shares, thus increasing the risk factor; (2) he usually has to pay above the market price, which reduces the potential return; (3) his action must have an effect on the rest of his "portfolio"—that is, a bad buy will pull down the valuation of the other assets in the company. At least our investment bad eggs don't spread infection.

For those who welcome sturdy corporate independence, the ability of companies to make their bids in paper, sometimes without even seeking the approval of stockholders, is abhorrent. Unquestionably, the amount of acquisitions would drop sharply and permanently if acquirers could purchase only for cash. The mere fact that a company can proceed with a cash bid out of its own resources is some small guarantee of its own viability. Firms might still raise cash to finance their corporate buys, but in that event their plans would be scrutinized by the financial institutions that would have to provide the currency. But unfortunately, here the true interests of the shareholder as investor cut across the artificial interests of the shareholder as taxpayer: the capital gains tax makes investors opt for shares, on which no tax need be paid (at least yet awhile), rather than cash, from which the taxable element of their profit has to be deducted.

But remember one of our golden rules. Never do anything foolish for sensible tax reasons. If a decision makes no sense with all tax considerations pushed to one side, then it very probably makes no sense, period. You know the rule: would I buy this stock (the one you're being offered in exchange for your own) at the present market price? And you also know the correct response if the answer is No—you don't stay with the new stock if the deal goes through. You sell out as soon as may be and pay the tax.

That's one of the safest guidelines in the whole postwar investment game. The wise ones were seldom those who stayed with either company in a big merger. Both the birds in the hand and those in the bush, far more often than not, go to those who have the sense to take their money and run.

19 When the Watchdog's Asleep, Learn to Bark

A trail of frauds and failures, confidence tricks and gross speculation, peculation and hocus-pocus helped to undermine investor confidence in the 1960s, paving the way for general financial breakdown. The process is self-reinforcing. Each scandal undermines the nerve of the investing public on which the industry ultimately depends, and not just the nerve, but the financial muscle. The investors who dropped a bundle in Investors Overseas Services, or got caught in the downfall of Lewis Gilbert's enterprises, or bought any of the hot stocks which suddenly entered their own private icebox, simply had less funds to put back into the market, even if they still wanted to revisit the scene of their downfall. More important, the scandals were the outward and visible signs of the inner corruption eating away at the health and structure of markets. Yet none of those watchdogs who were supposed to stop 1929 recurring flickered a muscle while all this evidence was unfolding beneath their eyes.

True, certain rules were laid down to ensure that

fool's gold couldn't be sold under a label saying that the gold was authentic. But if people chose to buy fool's gold for a true gold price, that was their foolish fault. Every authority should have known that the plethora of schemes for collective investment in real estate were bound to collapse, because they were based on the untenable proposition that real-estate values would always advance, year in, year out. The watchdogs, however, proved no wiser than the American banks, which were stuck in the autumn of 1975 with $11 billion in loans to Real Estate Investment Trusts, with which they also shared $15 billion of noninterest-bearing loans on property. One of the few near-certain laws of economic life is that all rises eventually reverse, but you have to be brave as well as wise to voice the warnings of Cassandra while all the Trojans around are sure they will thrash the Greeks.

The real-estate venturers had created their own illusory currency—constantly appreciating, yet inflation-proof; both solid and liquid. In exactly the same way the securities industry manufactured another spurious store of wealth: our old friend, the growth stock, whose price bore no relation to current real values (so far as these could be determined), because only future values (which couldn't be determined at all) counted.

Even if the regulators had wanted to check the abuses, they would have had the problem of identifying the wrongdoing, or even the wrongdoers. The outward and visible offenders were the shortcut villains who always emerge when the public is being taken for a costly ride. The buck can never be fast enough for them. Since selling genuine earnings to the public at an inflated price takes too long, the villains simply manufacture false profits. That criminal act can be identified

and punished: *deliberately* producing shoddy investment goods is a crime. But what about *selling* them?

In law there is no extra culpability when a broker
sells a share whose value turns out to be based on fraud
and deceit; the blame is no more than is attached to
promoting a stock on future earnings prospects which
don't materialize. The fatal flaw is that the investment
industry has a vested interest in believing the stories
it is told. Fast action in fast-climbing stocks produces
fast profits, in commissions and dealing gains. But this
chain reaction only needs to be broken once (as the
fall in real-estate values broke the chain of confidence
in property funds) for the profitable game to end.

Much of the investment world has been steeped in
the psychology of boom up to and beyond its necks. So
though a broker may advise you that the market, either
in general or for some particular stock, is too high for
the present, if he goes on to tell you that it won't or
shouldn't ever see that height again, the basic psychology of the market is under threat.

The watchdogs are there to protect us from
criminals—at which they were no great shakes in the
sixties; to defend the weak from the strong—ensuring
that minority shareholders get equal treatment, for
instance; and even to protect fools from their folly—to
some limited extent. Thus, curbs on stock market credit
helped to save the investor from the worst financial
disaster of all—losing more than he had invested. To
be partly wiped out is better than to be totally
destroyed.

But the watchdogs slept too often and too deeply.
Fantastically enough, lax administration of the rules
laid down for financial solidity on Wall Street was

allowed to bring the New York Stock Exchange perilously close to collapse.

A country's economic health really does depend in part on a healthy stock market, much to the annoyance of left-wing economists. The market value of a company's stock is a crucial constituent of its ability to borrow money and so to invest. It also affects the level of personal wealth throughout the economy, or at least the perceived level of wealth, and so affects willingness to spend.

A prolonged slump in the market produces falls in other barometers of confidence, with a general lowering effect on business activity, and there is a greater gathering of gloom still as the investments held as loan security start to collapse below the value of the loans—both lender and borrower suddenly find their backs to the financial wall.

That's why Richard Nixon, like Herbert Hoover before him, felt bound to advise Americans to buy common stocks at a time when every consideration of economic self-interest demanded that investors should retreat from the market in full flood—which they continued to do. The citizen has long since learned to ignore the financial advice of politicians. The soft touch that the Nixon Administration brought to the management of the Securities and Exchange Commission, its main watchdog, was another factor in the debacle. This behavior was wholly consistent with the President's general attitude to regulatory agencies and the welfare of businessmen, but in the climate of 1968-72 it was as dangerous as an unexploded bomb.

Even if the SEC had set out to return the markets of the post-sixties to sanity, the difficulties would have been stupendous; and the more the regulators had tried to regulate, the worse their problems, simply because the weight of the work load was beyond the lifting powers of bureaucratic man. The SEC, in any event, has to administer detailed laws—so detailed that meeting its disclosure requirements involves an immense and (for the ordinary investor) impenetrable mass of words.

Disclosure is not enough. Time and again we have the ridiculous charade of the Empty Chalice: a company comes to market on a prospectus that declares honestly that the product isn't yet in production, the market for it may not exist, the technical difficulties (which are intense) have not been overcome, there is no management ability whatsoever, nor adequate finance, and if, by some miracle, the whole thing works, the directors will pour most of the gravy over their own meat. The SEC will duly allow this farrago to come to market. But forewarned is not forearmed: the licensing of such offerings is indefensible.

The quality of disclosure, too, is as vital as its quantity—probably more so. Accountancy is a game of interpretation; the regulators cannot reasonably be expected to check through every set of accounts, fine print, thick language and all, as carefully as the auditors of the company. There would be neither time, nor in most cases necessity. Which is why the SEC could claim to be regulating a situation in which, say, National Student Marketing Corporation gaily included in its profits those of acquisitions made after the end of the financial year.

NSMC, what's more, issued blatantly misleading statements, all of which served to boost the share price, without anybody's knuckles getting rapped until far too late in the day, when the company had collapsed. Mal-

feasance is brought to the authorities' notice by mis-
adventure, rarely by vigilance. So the investor receives
the attentions not of a physician or surgeon, who might
manage a cure, but of an undertaker and gravedigger.

In the City of London, the bureaucratic failings
of the SEC have not gone unnoticed. Not because The
City wants to produce a better regulatory agency, free
of the SEC's defects, but because it wants passionately
to avoid any official regulation at all. Britain, like
America, has laws against financial frauds of various
kinds, but these laws share the principal defect of the
mills of the gods in that they grind exceeding slow,
while lacking the virtue of those mills, which also
grind exceeding sure.

The idea that The City should regulate itself, free
of the attentions of outsiders who may not share the
same gentlemanly code, is another of the charming
antique survivals of English life, like the beefeaters in
the Tower. The flavor of the code can be tasted from
one grimy episode in which a former Lord Mayor of
London, Sir Denys Lowson, was found to have made
some £5 million of personal profit by selling assets to a
public company under his control for far more than
they had recently cost him. With howls of fury echo-
ing around his head, Sir Denys (whose death saved
him from ultimate disgrace) announced that he would
surrender his "fair and reasonable" loot, "in accordance
with the best interests of the City of London." Making
profits by illicitly exploiting an inside position is thus
defensible: giving them up when you are found out
conforms with the unwritten code.

Those who rely on insiders to police their own
patches have the kind of temperament that fancies
walks by night in Central Park. The well-being of in-

vestors always comes into the equation, of course, since bilked investors are rotten customers. But the main weight of regulation leads not to the protection of the investor, but to that of the securities industry. That was the historic origin of the SEC in the United States: without Roosevelt's reforms, the investment industry would have been unable to resume its rudely interrupted function. By giving the public confidence in the honesty of the markets and the soundness of the wares they offered, the laws made the sale of stocks possible, even to a generation which remembered vividly the havoc caused by the overselling and underprotection of the past.

The recognizable abuses can be legislated against and punished, if not prevented. But there is a more generalized, more insidious, far more expensive abuse, that of letting perversion of values burgeon, so long as it isn't founded on outright criminality; this abuse has no redress, and certainly no prevention. Possibly no prevention exists. If some authority were to take courage in both hands and to declare that at a price-earning ratio of 40 not only IBM but any stock is overvalued, would the investing public react with any more sense of self-protection than a smoker notified on each package of the government's health warning?

The job of regulators is to try to stop the investor being flagrantly cheated, not to prevent him from paying over the hypothetical odds. Any other policy would negate the purpose of regulation, which, as we saw, is to enable markets to flourish. But the twin objectives—acting when criminality or deception is suspected, but making no moves that might disrupt the ordinary business of the investment community—were among the good intentions with which the road to the stock market hell of the early seventies was paved.

When, after the debacle, the SEC became more active, the dilemma immediately reared its head. The SEC felt that banks, when soliciting new funds, should include the bald and horrific facts about that eleven billions of dud loans to the Real Estate Investment Trusts. The Federal Reserve Board, which was supposed to regulate the banks, objected strenuously to this demand, on the grounds that disclosure would undermine the public's increasingly fragile confidence in the banking system.

The interests of the individual investor, who might subscribe to the bank issues, and surely had a right to know about the large, uncovered, and irrecoverable debts, were, in the mind of the Fed, to be subjugated to the rights of the wider community, which didn't want its banks to cave in.

Concentration on wrongdoing and not rocking the investment industry's boat leaves the investor with scant protection—even against criminals. Since there has to be a fire before there is any smoke, the regulators don't move until the blaze is under way; their action, once it becomes public, destroys the market value of the shares —if any remains. More often than not, the horse has already bolted—and the stable door remains wide open for other escapes with other people's money.

Doctors are supposed to pass exams to prove that they know the difference between the vermiform appendix and the small colon; lawyers likewise are expected not to land their clients in bankruptcy by oversight. Both can (with great difficulty) be prosecuted for professional failure. But any fool can float a public company (and many do), and any other fool can pass the shares off at incredible prices to a credulous public —and nobody can be taken to legal task.

Even auditors, professional men to the fingertips, have been able to claim immunity after passing the accounts of companies whose finances would not have deceived Little Orphan Annie. If the auditors stumble across the fact that the company has less than no hope of receiving any cash for an alleged sale, they will pursue the matter. If they don't spot the weakness, the missing millions are not their affair, but that of the board. The directors in turn can plead the best of managerial intentions, or possibly the worst of managerial misjudgments, either one a possible source of stockholder suits, but neither a hanging matter. And if the burden on directors becomes too onerous, people will refuse to serve on boards: the money isn't enough to compensate for the inconvenience of being sued, or of trying to avoid that fate.

The market, its defenders say, is inherently speculative: those who gamble on stocks and shares, like those who bet on horses, mustn't be surprised if they lose from time to time; all the authorities can do is prevent the runners being doped or otherwise hobbled, and this is rarely achieved before the race starts.

But if the stock markets do play the crucial part in the economy that we have outlined, they matter far more than horse races, just as the savings of a lifetime are more important than a $10 bet. Yet the men who run companies, promote securities and sell them to the public are not licensed in the sense of other professionals; they merely have license. In the speculative orgy of the sixties, it proved to be like that of Ian Fleming's James Bond: a license to kill.

When the Watchdog's Asleep, Learn to Bark

Take the matter of insider trading; all good men and true, together with several bad men and false, deplore, despise and deprecate the practice. No professional misconduct, short of outright theft of a customer's securities, is more likely to bring on permanent disapproval and blackballing by the Establishment than that of the Inside Crook. Yet hardly a professional breathes who has never used inside information for his own inclusive benefit. To expect anything else demands too much from the natural condition of economies, markets and mankind.

The issue is far less clear-cut than the average burglary. Certainly the director, manager, accountant or lawyer who uses to his profit secret information gathered in the course of his duties is a thief—just as is the store manager who accepts a kickback from a supplier. When Texas Gulf Sulphur made its unlikely find of an Eldorado of silver and zinc at Timmins, Ontario, its executives might conceivably have been wise to keep the discovery private for the good of the company's business. They were unquestionably sinful to add to their personal piles of shares while the news was still in their private possession. Those robbed were the investors from whom the executives bought their additional shares. Had the Timmins lode been public knowledge, those investors would never have sold—at least not at the price at which they were robbed.

That ranked high among the scandals which should have alerted the powerful authorities of America to the fact that the hectic stock markets of the sixties were seething with symptomatic corruption. The markets bubbled with inside information and inside activity. Chairmen attempted to push up the price of their stock; public relations departments were instructed to pump up the price with any hot air available. Executives with large stock options were under constant pressure to deliver, privately or publicly, the good news that might turn their castles in Spain into yachts off Florida.

The professionals in the markets were, and are, eager customers for nuggets of good news. All professional investment is governed by the ceaseless search for information. The difference lies in what kind of information is sought. Type A knowledge, for example, is as innocent as a newborn company: knowledge that may or may not affect the market price, like the good word that current trading is exceptionally fine, or that second quarter profits will be 27.6% higher. One of the several necessary delusions under which the Securities and Exchange Commission operates is that it performs a valuable duty by insisting that Type A news be shared at once with the American public. The truth, nine times out of ten, is that neither you, I nor anybody else knows which way the market will turn on such tidings.

If the price rises, onlookers will wisely attribute the advance to the second quarter forecast. If the price falls, the same sages will remark that the market had been "discounting" good second quarter earnings for some time past. "Discounting" is one of the excuse words which serve wrong-footed experts uncommonly well at all seasons. In a bad season, anyway, reports of higher profits will probably make no headway against the prevailing tides. At times during the Second Great Crash, even the announcement of an oil strike on Staten Island would have left a great petroleum combine with stone-cold stock.

Similarly, in good seasons all news is grist to the mill, because the pros are hungry for any excuse to make the mill grind faster. The individual investor is thus highly unlikely to be bilked by lack of access to Type A information. But as a point of sober fact, few fortunes are made on this Type A route. Directors are notoriously bad judges of the value of their own companies' stock. Most company insiders are unlikely to be in difficulty over Type A information; even if it were a gift horse, they would look it in the mouth without hesitation. Probably most executives are too overcome by the cares of managing to spare much time for their investments, which is possibly one of the reasons why the American executive so eagerly embraces the stock option, which does his investment thinking for him—and on the cheap.

Executives who are innocents in the ways of the market are unlikely to let fall from their mouths anything of much use to the recipients. Urging all listeners to purchase their company's shares because of their sublime cheapness hardly adds up to inside information, and hardly ever amounts to good advice, for that matter. Perversely enough, the exceptions—where the shares truly are cheap, undervalued by the criteria of past and present alike—tend to stay exceptional. They are cheap for a reason—such as the belief by powerful investors that the presiding genius is a thief. He may never have thieved, but no amount of inside information will erase the image and shift the market status of the shares.

As a rough (very rough) rule for your thumb, the stock with an amazing record whose share price and price-earnings ratio have *always* been earthbound is a much safer investment than that whose stock market rating, after years of flying high, suddenly but firmly refuses to respond to the chairman's zest—and is thus promptly labeled a bargain. Stock market tipsters, however, tend to fall for the latter shares much more easily—just like most investors. They thus disobey the most important law of inside information: its existence and possession only matter when action is taken on that inside knowledge. If a share misbehaves itself in an inexplicable manner, somebody else must be buying, or selling, on a significant scale—and perhaps, as in the case of Texas Gulf Sulphur, for a significant reason.

If this is so, the proud possessors are almost certainly using Type B information, the kind that will unquestionably affect the shares: like the news that some uninstructed multinational is about to pay four times the going price for the stock. Those who profit from privileged or surefire Type B information to plume their own nests are worthy of scorn, hatred and fear, no less than those (often the same people) who use their power to manipulate shares exclusively for their own benefit.

The manipulators deserve hatred because every penny of their profit has been garnered at the expense of weaker (i.e., less favored) and probably poorer brethren. But the real fear is not for them—very few, if any, of history's sharp market crooks ever amounted to much—but rather that their corruption will undermine the market. Markets, including stock exchanges, make the difference between a free and a controlled economy. The overwhelming case against the manipulators is that they control or rig what is supposed to be free, and so jeopardize its continued existence.

But the philosophy of free enterprise is remote from the realities of markets and from the practical difficulties of determining inside from outside, right from wrong. The tricky act of divorcing the investment interests from the banking sides, and keeping the latter's information from seeping into the former's consciousness, has long been a specialty of the London merchant banks. A client fell to earth in a welter of shareholders' blood; the bank that advised the company was miraculously found to have rid its trusts in the nick of time of once large holdings of the afflicted stock; yet outsiders were supposed to believe that the investment managers had moved entirely on the promptings of their inner wisdom, without even consulting the banking colleagues who were close to the crumbling company. According to the authorized version, in one such case, the bankers were unaware of the full impending calamity; their comrades, on the other hand, had picked up the scent of disease with nothing but twitching nostrils. Thus both sides of the bank had perfectly clean hands to wash.

Those who can believe that story have truly touching faith. Not that belief or disbelief is of any account in this context. Nobody, by the lights of the City of London, had misbehaved. By the lights of Wall Street, or at least of the Securities and Exchange Commission, the incident would have attracted attention and possibly action. The SEC's eagle eye alights even on some small, if significant, corners of alleged inside malpractice. For instance, the SEC claimed that two Metro-Goldwyn-Mayer financial decisions had been motivated by the desire to help one Kirk Kerkorian pay off his bank loans. MGM's helpfulness would not have been discouraged by the fact that Kerkorian is vice-chairman and principal stockholder.

The SEC has also latterly been taking a jaundiced view of brokerage houses and banks whom it suspects of acting on adverse information before the general public had a chance. Favored clients with large future funds to invest are the first people an investment house would want to tip off when one of its herds starts producing sour milk. Yet a nod, a wink or an eloquent silence can achieve the same result as a leak—and for every deliberate indiscretion that the SEC suspects, or can prove, a thousand others go unnoticed and unpoliced.

One defense for the outsider would be to prohibit those who manage public companies from owning any equity in either their own firm or any other with which it has business dealings. The ban isn't without precedent: executives are not supposed, for example, to own undeclared interests in firms that trade with their own, otherwise the temptation to negotiate especially large and gratifying contracts with themselves might become irresistible.

But capitalism is built by capitalists. You can hardly separate the capitalist from his capital without destroying the system, any more than, without changing their function altogether, you can prevent investment banks from taking stakes in companies in which they are or might be interested.

Since the law can only intervene like the cop on the beat—when there is an indication of sin—the main guarantee of good inside behavior from insiders, under the existing rules, is their own integrity. When any financial market reaches the point where the only limit to gain is the extent of the insider's own greed, however, eventual disaster is written on the wall. In the good old days, the theory was that elder statesmen of the utmost propriety would protect the greedy man from his own greed, and thus safeguard the interests of the outsiders. But such graybeards were probably always less common than the theory maintained.

Today, the cult of performance has removed the last barrier to naked avarice. After all, if the object of the company is to maximize its financial horsepower, any device that guns up the engine can only serve the cult, enriching the insider, true, but incidentally benefiting the other shareholders as well. The blotch on this picture of mutual, if somewhat one-sided, profit is that riches grown by artificial means are bound to wither before the chill breath of reality.

Paper fortunes made by promoters evaporated in mere weeks when the cold wind blew. After all, if Company A sold its stake in Company B to Company C, which A also controlled, for a huge profit, where had the additional wealth been created? Since the answer was nowhere, some of the people had been fooled all of the time. But they positively wanted to be fooled; the nature of the deception was, for a time, to increase their own paper wealth. The affection of investors for men who make them rich is so intense that it will even survive a series of body blows to the wallet. Still, the unacceptable faith that outsiders repose in those inside cannot be fully explained by pecuniary interest. The loyalty of stock market fans who remain faithful through fire and water probably expresses psychological necessity. The act of confiding money to a company is an act of dedication. The faith becomes transferred, like the sexual affections of the analysand to the analyst, to the human personifications of the investment.

If the Freudian argument holds any water, the analogy can be taken a stage further. The profit-producing inside genius becomes a father figure to the investor. He has thrust onto another person the responsibility of caring for his money. Having done the transference, the last thing he wants is to admit that the chosen figure has failed him—by not feathering the stockholder's nest, or by placing far too much plumage in his own. Lord Thomson, the Canadian newspaper and broadcasting proprietor, used to tell employees, "You make a buck for me, and I'll make a buck for you." Corporate outsiders say to those inside, "You make a buck for me, and I don't care if you make ten for yourself."

If that's your attitude, it opens the way, not only to arrant sentimentality, but to exploitation. Remember that an investment is simply a deposit of money that should stay where you have placed it only for so long as no better home comes to your attention. You owe nothing to the managements of companies, especially if they have failed you, and above all if their failure consists of using their inside position for personal gain. The managers are paid to manage; what happens to their personal fortunes above and beyond their salaries should be subject to the same rules and limitations that apply to your treasure.

You have no option but to accept the fact that ninety-nine times out of a hundred, you're on the outside looking in; that those on the inside looking out are in a far better position to protect their interests; and that only in rare instances (for example, when a powerful and wealthy shareholder happens to dislike what's going on) will you as outsider get any effective support from any source save heaven. The only safe course is to invest solely on results, not reputation, and to behave in general like the celebrated detective of fiction who, asked whom he suspected, looked darkly around the room and whispered to the inquirer: "Everybody."

Again, ninety-nine times out of a hundred nobody will be deliberately trying to defraud you. The deliberate defrauder sets out to part people from real wealth in exchange for objects, or apparent objects, which are either worth much less than the price paid, or worth nothing at all—and there's no better or richer field for such activities than the sale of securities.

Securities, after all, are mere pieces of paper—a description that applies to shares in American Telephone & Telegraph as accurately as to a title to nonexistent land in the Bahamas. And it takes a particularly sharp-eyed watchdog to distinguish between dishonest and genuine embossed certificates. Even true certificates might be false: in modern times felons like Lewis M. Gilbert, for instance, raised badly needed wind by issuing securities that were not backed by the assets to which they were legally entitled.

So long as the supporters of a Gilbert believed the shares had full worth, and hung on to the paper, no harm could befall. But any efforts to dispose of the watered stock inevitably undermine the financial basis of the whole corporation. The principle is the same as that of the man who sells the same house twice to two different people. The scheme is perfect so long as one of the victims never seeks to claim his property.

Many other approaches have been taken to the ungentle art of parting us from our money, ranging from the misappropriation of insurance premiums to the creation of assets out of thinnest air. But these operations, like watering the stock, involve criminal acts and, when detected, will be punished by the criminal law. Most of the historic scandals have fallen into this category. The Swedish match king Ivar Kreuger sold the same bonds again and again; the salad oil swindler Tino de Angelis borrowed money on the security of salad oil that wasn't there; the French financier Serge Stavisky did his borrowing on the strength of forged pawnbroking tickets. Like Lewis M. Gilbert, they either ended up in jail, or avoided that fate by the bullet (Kreuger's and Stavisky's end), or by exile (Brazil is still playing host to several refugees from the Securities and Exchange Commission).

The sixties and seventies saw several collapses that were the match for the celebrated crashes between the wars. The fall of Bernie Cornfeld's Investors Overseas Services, like its previous global spread, was the equal of the Kreuger destruction. The crumbling of the Sindona banking empire can be spoken of in the same breath as the Stavisky *affaire* (it even had political overtones). These were only two of the top-ranking investor disasters of the epoch. Scandal followed scandal, but scandal wasn't always met with judicial retribution. By 1975, the only punishment meted out to Bernie Cornfeld after the 1968 collapse of IOS was a prolonged spell in a Swiss jail before and without trial. Neither he nor any of his minions paid any other personal penalty for carryings-on that cost the investing public of the world millions. The IOS practitioners had lawyers and legal devices to ensure that at all times they kept to the right side of the law, however narrow the margin of legal safety. And the lax or nonexistent regulation of offshore trusts by onshore governments greatly helped the process of keeping within legitimate bounds. But the false goods sold by IOS were intrinsically safe in the legal sense: the fund's founders sold what they *said* they were selling. The lies lay mostly in their promises, rather than their properties.

If the charges that IOS levied for its management services were excessive, and if the money paid over to the Cornfeld treasury earned large dollops of cash for Cornfeld & Co. before being invested, at least the charges were relatively open and at least the money was invested where IOS said it would be. The buyer had the chance to beware. If he chose to be pressured into paying Cornfeld fees, that was his problem. After all, some people prefer paying delicatessen prices to shopping in supermarkets, and on their own heads be it.

Admittedly, the situation changed when IOS began investing in its own in-house funds instead of other people's. But these investments, too, however ill-advised, were at least made; and the egregious errors of the Cornfeld managers in buying beaten-up, no-hope growth stars and unregistered securities of doubtful status were committed by other investment managers by the score. Even when the IOS instigators cashed in their own chips by selling shares in the management company, the operation was no different in principle than other offers for sale of go-go outfits at the peak of their prosperity and fame. Only a charitable ninny sells out below the crest of the wave.

What were the IOS crimes, after all? When floating the company, the promoters had, it later appeared, overstated the profits. But they operated in an era when all concerned were expected to lend a hand in boosting the figure *on* the bottom line, which in turn could elevate the crucial number—earnings per share. As for selling IOS securities to the public on the basis of forecasts that later proved to be hopelessly optimistic, that too was a common event of the epoch. The essence of forecasts is that they may be wrong. The future is not a fact, but a supposition, and in the great majority of cases where promoters failed to meet their promises, the failure was genuine. They themselves truly believed that the sensational momentum of their past growth would continue.

IOS was continually begging journalists to fly out to Vevey to admire, not just the Cornfeld bevy of beautiful girls, but also the perfection of their managements systems—even though one consultant, unable to find any evidence of system at all, had returned to California after telling the IOS moguls of his lack of discovery. The mob persisted in its self-deception until the fall of the house confirmed the consultant's findings. Money was gushing out of the company, under nobody's control, and without anybody taking care or thought to see that the next year's, month's, week's or day's bills could be paid. Even the basic simplicities of financial control were not honored.

Some of the architects of the jerry-built empires of this period may have known all too well what they were doing. The overstatement of profits, the cooking of books in the tastiest sauce available, the false (but legally impeccable) prospectuses, the mismanagement which diverted cash to known and unknown destinations: all these could fit as easily into a cunning, deliberate plot to defraud as into a picture of incompetence magnified by greed.

In history as in everyday life, however, it doesn't follow that because the conspiracy theory fits the facts, a conspiracy exists. In many cases the criminal and near-criminal deceivers of the period blundered into their deceits. The authors of the Equity Funding insurance scandal did not start out in business with the intention of reinsuring phony policies made out on the lives of phony people. The device was introduced later, when other ways of maintaining the company's handsome investment profile were flagging.

But the Equity excesses grew out of the pursuit

of supernormal growth in earnings per share, which was itself the supreme excess. It drove operators across the line that separates honest dishonesty from the dishonest kind: from being uncatchable to being caught. The line between innocent ignorance on the one side and knowing fraud on the other is difficult to draw, and this difficulty is the main reason why a new kind of scandal, the disappearance of millions in savings with no hope of redress or civilized revenge, has come to loom larger than the huge organized frauds of earlier generations. The scandalous task is made easier, moreover, because society in the shape of the State cares little about the milking of the citizenry—so long as no legally defined crime has been committed in the process.

The rewards can be far higher than those of common or garden larceny. A thief seldom finds a couple of million lying about, as in the Great Train Robbery or the Brinks' raid. But the market capitalizations of public companies are so large even in bad times that the sale of a quarter of an inflated equity can yield a sum beyond the dreams of any bank robber.

The point of weakness, as in all frauds, is that at which we part with our money. We naked investors have no guarantee that any of the numbers on which we might base our judgment of the purchase are what they purport to be. The dividend may not in reality be coming out of cash earnings; the earnings may not be the surplus actually generated from the sales made in the current year; the sales reported for the current year may not have been completed; the costs deducted from those sales may not be the whole costs; there may be liabilities looming ahead of which nothing has been reported, possibly even suspected. We have no real means of knowing whether the managers of the company are crooks or honest beavers, idle or intelligent, always on the premises or mostly in Florida.

In most cases the stocks will cause no more injury than the market as a whole inflicts. But the inherent deficiencies of the deal easily allow the dishonest to exploit the exposed position of the purchaser. Their tool is the price-earnings multiple. So long as a dollar of earnings can be changed into $5, or $10, or $20, or (to return to the sixties) $100, the company promoter has a license to print money. Since the money is spurious, however, the time must come when its true value reasserts itself, and the shareholders are left holding an empty bag.

The crooks and the self-deceivers could never pull off their new kinds of scandal without the enthusiastic cooperation of others who may not even be cut in on the deal: the stockbrokers and other retailers of shares; the big institutions and the professions; the banks and investment funds that finance and invest in the scandalous companies; the auditors who manage to find a thousand reasons why they can allow certain advantageous but highly arguable methods of accountancy to be applied; the lawyers who help to devise deals that have the effect of benefiting the directors at the expense of the shareholders; the academics and consultants who feed the vanity and the appetites of the unbridled expansionist with inflated, false concepts; even the media that insist on creating heroes in a business and management world where Olympian figures are even rarer than in the arts.

As the pieces of the Second Great Crash were being picked up, the accountancy profession in particular started to repair the damage its members had done to us, sometimes inadvertently, but often just as devastatingly as if they had actually intended to weaken our trust in the system.

Quite apart from their belated discovery that inflation overstates company profits, the accountants came out with a number of tightened rules. After long years of investor abuse, they finally decided that it was wrong to capitalize research and development instead of charging the spending against current income. For all those years, the argument had been faithfully trotted out that the R and D was a source of future profit, just like a new piece of plant, and that its capitalization was no different in kind than that of fixed investment in machinery. But in 1974 the American Institute of Certified Public Accountants took a closer look and came up with an extraordinary conclusion.

"Evidence of a direct causal relationship between current research and development expenditures and subsequent future benefits generally has not been found," said the accountants. "Even an indirect cause and effect relationship can seldom be demonstrated." That being so, what were the accountants of America up to when they allowed company after company to proceed on exactly the opposite assumption, declaring current profits when in many cases none existed? Shouldn't they have made the inquiries that resulted in the 1974 verdict long before?

Ah-ha, they can reply, companies that treated their R and D as a contribution from the great hereafter were compelled by law or their auditors or both to inform shareholders of the practice. If the investors failed to read the notes, or having read them, to take any notice, that was their problem.

This convenient formula glossed over the fact that

there's no reason why most of us members of the saving population should be, financially speaking, in the literacy class of the accountant. Even the meaning of "capitalizing R and D," let alone its significance, would escape many of us completely. *Caveat emptor* in these circumstances makes about as much sense as printing "Poison —Not to Be Taken" on liniment distributed exclusively to homes for the blind.

The door that is swung open by *caveat emptor* is no different from that through which lesser con men force their entrance. But in any human arena, it's a great mistake to underestimate the ultimate shrewdness of man. Indeed, all circular cons (in which succeeding investors pay their predecessors, and the con man takes his slice from the top) eventually founder when the supply of gullible investors runs out. The new kinds of scandal that emerged in the world's stock markets ran the same risk. The Penn Central Railroad, W. T. Grant's stores, Burmah Oil, Rolls-Royce: these were not inventions of fly-by-night promoters, but apparently solid, gilt-edged companies into which an investor might stash his money, and sleep safely o' nights. Their setbacks, ranging from complete collapse to total loss of confidence, helped to remove billions in buying power from the investors of the West. Between 1972 and 1974, some $60 billion of equity values disappeared in London alone: something like $1200 per man, woman and child in the population.

Maybe the number of public companies has simply become too large for effective policing. Maybe the variables in double-entry bookkeeping are simply too many for any hard-and-fast rules capable of covering all eventualities to be drawn up. Maybe the equity-buying classes are too unimportant politically to be worth the attention of the rest of the community. Maybe so: but the fact remains that those pieces of paper being exchanged represent the real industrial wealth of the community. The investor, in that sense, is a representative of society as a whole. If we are cheated, then so is the community. It's high time that all of us were better protected, for all of our sakes.

20 Money Isn't Everything – Unless It's Yours

So far, we've kept as far away as possible from the microeconomics of the firm and management theory, and for good reason. All you should care about is the present and future value of any investment you are thinking of buying (or selling); and we've established, again and again, that the causal links between economic or managerial performance and the performance of your money are too tenuous, winding and obscure for you, or anybody else, to unravel. But the time has come for a brief dip into microeconomics: the theory of the big company.

That's because big companies attract most of the attention in the investment world. This is less because of their looming power on the economic scene than because, if the stock market is considered as a casino, they supply the overwhelming majority of the chips. If the game is to be one for many players, the rest of us have no option but to play with the big-company chips. They are the only ones in large enough supply to go around. Indeed, the ratio between the Goliaths and the

Davids is among the more awesome discrepancies in world finance.

But saying that it would cost two or three billion to buy U.S. Steel is, in a manner of speaking, a grand euphemism. Financial reporters are fond of saying that so many millions have been wiped off the value of a company's shares because of some natural calamity (like forgetting to count the inventory). But the loss is purely on paper, which is as true of the market capitalization: it is just a paper calculation. The market can only value what is actually on the market. Even in a loosely held company, only a small part of the shares will be available or potentially available at any time; a major chunk of the equity may be tied up as securely as a Christmas parcel.

This isn't necessarily because some founding family is clasping the shares to its bosom. A large, inert body of shareholders always exists: institutions and individuals who for some reason, or for no reason, regard their holdings as precious heirlooms, never to be disturbed.

By and large, however, institutions are somewhat less likely to take permanent, unreasoning shines to a stock, and their presence is much more marked among the big battalions. From the viewpoint of supply and demand, the individual shareholder should be on their side, especially since the received view at all times in the second half of the twentieth century has been that the large corporations, however undynamic in stock exchange performance, will inherit the economic earth.

The race has gone, in market after market, to the competitors who can spread their costs over the largest and longest product runs; and at the retail end, to those who can buy and distribute in the greatest quantities.

Not only are there economies of scale in production and distribution, but management, if theory means anything, should reap a like benefit. One brilliant man handling $100 million sales should earn at least ten times the profit of an equally clever executive with only $10 million turnover to exploit. And the extra financial muscle bulging in the first fellow's biceps, both in terms of cash flow and borrowing power, will turn an edge into an overwhelming and irreversible advantage.

But theory only means as much as practice will allow. It doesn't follow, even in theory, that economies of scale are subject to no ceiling at all.

In management, this phenomenon is well established and well understood. Above a certain size—some say 200, some 500, some 1000—factory employment passes beyond the ability of one ace to control and direct effectively. No matter how excellent he is, the task has expanded beyond his span. The larger the company gets, the more layers of management have to be inserted between top and bottom, which means, often enough, that the superman at the summit isn't engaged in any activity that could truly be called managing.

But if the economies of mass management are a chimera, few people, even today, have queried those of mass production, although in one of the world's most conspicuous markets—automobiles—the middling firms like Peugeot, B.M.W. and Volvo have consistently confounded the giants like General Motors, Ford, Volkswagen and Fiat, whose million-car runs should have carried all before them—in theory.

In fact, a paper delivered in 1972 by two Shell International Chemical experts at a conference in Bratislava not only queries the benefits of massive scale, it demolishes them. The experts argued that every giant chemical maker in the world (and few such firms are not gigantic) built plants well above the optimum size (partly because they ignored costs and considerations that would have spoiled the proleviathan sums). Since all the giants were building these "monuments to megalomania" simultaneously, they also guaranteed a condition of oversupply that savaged their prices and profits beyond short-term repair.

Of course they stayed in business. But this saving grace of the great company is its underlying weakness: the *diseconomy* of scale in the matter of wealth which allows companies to absorb horrendous difficulties and pretend almost that they have never happened.

From the manager's angle, that is a consoling ability. But for us naked investors, the cushioning of mistakes, the making of losses and the sterile commitment of capital, add up to a running disaster. The price of the great company's absorption powers is that the return on *our capital*, the source of all goodness, remains stuck in the nether regions.

Consider the case of Du Pont. Sales in 1974 came to $6.9 billion, or $18.9 million every working and weekend day. Even after all costs, interest and taxes had been lopped off, the company had $910.4 million left over in net profits and depreciation, or $2.5 million a day. If the company's comptrollers could contrive to delay payment of expenses ("costs of goods sold and other operating charges") for a day after receipt of income, its directors would have $13.9 million more to play with around the world. A week's delay adds up to no less than $97.3 million, on the 1974 figures.

Du Pont's numbers aren't especially gigantic. The British half of Royal Dutch-Shell, with only 40% of the group's worldwide sales, sold as much in pounds in 1974 as Du Pont did in dollars. For a company of Shell's size, losing $17 million in three years in partnership with the U.S. Armour giant in a forlorn effort to gain $40 million of United Kingdom fertilizer sales is a breeze. Even dropping $170 million, with equal futility, in nuclear energy isn't enough to spoil the boardroom luncheons.

The cash flow factor means that there is no practical limit to the grandiose plans which directors of the large companies in which we invest can form. Most such dignitaries will throw up their hands in horror at this juncture: to them life is a constant procession of schemes for which the capital can't be found—especially in the tight money conditions that accompanied the great fight against inflation.

But the argument overlooks two points: in the first place, "minor" expenditures, well into the millions, proceed without let or hindrance. And in the second place, the capital shortage arises partly because massive new plants have been piled upon the relative failure of equally superb monuments to past megalomania.

For instance, it's not surprising that Lockheed got strapped for cash for new projects as a result of the entirely predictable, and predicted, drain on its resources generated by the Tristar airliner. Yet, even though the Tristar was beyond Lockheed's financial powers, it could still proceed—foolishly, no doubt, but as inevitably as death or taxes; just as Chrysler was able to go on supporting its money-losing British subsidiary for years while its own equity capital (or, rather, *our* own capital) was being eaten up.

A high return on capital not only generates all goodness, as we noted, but is the source of all future capital:

self-generated or borrowed from outside. The illusions of big boards include the idea that borrowed money doesn't come from the company itself. Their self-deceptive thought is that the money goes into some wondrous asset, where it rests forever. So long as the investment generates an after-depreciation return which is higher than the interest paid on the borrowed money, and is sufficient to repay the capital, the company must win.

This forgets the catch that the asset must be replaced for far more than the depreciation money, and also overlooks the equally inconvenient fact that the investment often returns less than the interest cost. A twenty-year borrowing at 10% requires the generation of cash equal to 300% of the sum borrowed merely to take care of the interest and capital on the loan. Since the capital repayment has to be made post tax, that means a total return of 20% a year, and very few large companies have managed that for more than one glorious summer out of five.

But low returns on the capital they have already invested never stop managements of the mighty corporations from investing still more, in mammoth plants or in mergers. In theory the large company should have the resources of men and money, plus the know-how, to make its mergers work. In practice, however, big-company mergers take as long to succeed as elephants to gestate. And big-company buys often come unstuck —in part because they are mostly friendly, agreed affairs: giants don't like to be seen committing rape.

From mergers to marketing, money is only as much of an objective as the entrenched management cares to make it. At least investment spending is subject to all manner of controls, often needing board approval for all expenditure above a certain low limit. For some weird reason, money invested is considered holier than money spent on current account. At the very moment when a board is gravely deliberating whether to spend $250,000 on an extension to one of its plants, some unsupervised fellow is probably committing the company to an overspend of $2.5 million on a current item like materials.

When they do approve investments or other spending that turns out rotten, managers are only sometimes guilty of simple error or profligacy. In most cases, their motivation is the survival of the corporation. The sight of its defense business going out of the window inspired the management of Lockheed to seek civil salvation—and financial damnation—in the Tristar. The knowledge that one day mounting competition and market saturation would reduce the profitability of traditional lines led many managements, from RCA to Xerox, into the ruinous world of computers. Many studies have found that the perpetuation of the company, far more than any money motive, serves as the foundation of the managerial life and the true corporate philosophy of major groups.

But all this is of low interest to the naked investor. We want the company to survive only to the extent that we can cash in our chips whenever we want. From our point of view, the managerial idea of survival is no use—because survival is too easily contrived. So long as the management can maintain an adequate cash flow (which in any company of vast turnover is a relatively simple trick), the corporation can survive even with inadequate profits.

The shareholders might be better served if the business were trimmed down to its profitable elements, or sold off completely. The evidence shows that shareholders in trust-busted enterprises, like the former components of the Standard Oil Trust, fared much better after breakup than before—or than they could have expected if John D. Rockefeller's robber barony had remained intact. And it's hard to believe, for another example, that an integrated I. G. Farben chemical empire could have outperformed the three component parts into which it was split by the kindness of the Allies.

The picture is supported by the relatively dismal showing of big companies in the annual ten-year growth compilations published by *Fortune*. The diseconomies of scale clearly apply to growth potential as well. A big company seldom can grow at the pace of a small firm. Everything, even the mathematics, is against it.

The mathematical advantages a small company gets by beginning from near zero can't be easily distinguished from the inborn managerial assets which go with tininess. If money is tight, for example, it tends to be tightly used; if it happens to abound, the money will be used abundantly.

The smaller company has one other attraction for us when picking shares: at least the management's track record, if any, is visible. Nobody can even take a stab at judging the management caliber of the General Motors board. Even if (and it's doubtful) the chairman and the president really do run the company, their stay is so short, and our knowledge about their work beforehand so scanty, that the question isn't worth attempting. Who, after all, will reach for his checkbook on being informed that some character in his sixties, of whom he has heard nothing either good or bad, has been elected to the GM chair?

In the occasional years when a leviathan turns in bumper earnings, they can't be attributed to any one man or any group of men. And even when the track record is discernible, there is no guarantee that the past provides any guide to the future. Heroes of business and their corporate vehicles are, like man himself, born only to die.

Take as one case in a thousand the story of Playboy Enterprises, Inc. On the strength of a smashing record, Playboy went public in 1971; we investors snapped up a quarter of the shares for $23.50. Nobody suspected that the phenomenal ability of Hugh M. Hefner in magazine publishing was coupled with striking inability in everything else, including running clubs and hotels. Had Hefner proceeded with his 1975 plan to become private by buying back the shares, which had dropped to $3, the deal would have rubbed in the new robbery. A man who sells goods for $23.50 and buys them back, say, for $5, has made a profit of $18.50 from the deal.

If the investing public can go wrong judging a Hefner, whose works and ways are out in the comparative open, it hasn't a hope when it comes to one of the amorphous neoconglomerate managements that dominate the stock exchanges of the world. Nor can the investor now repose much faith in the traditional strengths of size. The Bratislava concept has even begun to break into the consciousness of big-company managers. In an age when small steel plants can be highly profitable, and large ones return minuscule yields, the penetration of management minds by the virtues of smallness is proceeding fast.

So from many angles, the big company seems a less safe refuge for investment money than in the past.

This raises an almost insoluble paradox. If the smallest companies include the best buys, yet there are not enough to go around, what is the investor, institutional or private, to do with his money? Was the ridiculous run-up in the price of alleged growth stocks in the sixties in part the reflection of too much of our money retreating from AT&T or Du Pont and plunging into too small a supply of the lesser-sized alternatives?

The situation could perhaps be resolved if the big companies reverted to the old gilt-edged, blue-chip status of which AT&T was once the prime example. Such an investment would be cash-rich: its managers would concentrate on paying bigger and bigger dividends in perfect safety year after year; they would distribute capital surpluses back to the stockholders; and growth in earnings per share would be as meaningless to their managements as the Koran. Above all, they would watch the spending of the shareholders' money with unremitting attention. To many big-company managements, seven-digit sums have become only money. But to the investor, it's only money—our money—that counts.

Which brings us to the crock of gold waiting at the end of the microeconomics. You'll rarely find a big-company investment with all the above characteristics. But make sure that those to which you entrust your wealth at least have that general configuration. If you take the trouble (as you should) to compare its previous two years' financial records, check that net cash (money at the bank and near money, like Treasury bills, minus short-term debt) rose between year ends. Look for evidence, too, that the dividend rises with earnings—and that the ratio paid out hasn't worsened to stockholders' disadvantage over the years. Watch the return on capital (*all* capital, not just the stockholders' equity) like a miser.

You can't change the system, but you can buck it. And if enough of us confine our interest to companies that truly look after our money, rather than guarding the management's self-esteem, we could—one day—change the system, too.

21 The Taxman Cometh On Strong

In the twenties private finance, then largely un-regulated by government, dug its own grave. In the sixties public finance, in an age when private money was under stricter public regulation than ever before, took on the role of irresponsibility. The profligacy of governments not only set the boom-and-bust going, but answers a more intriguing question: where the money went that disappeared in billions from the pockets of private investors. Most headed straight back to the governments from which it came.

From commodities to old masters, the surplus money unleashed by the governments of the West sought a limited supply of goods. The resulting inflation fed upon itself. The more prices rose, the more people attempted to protect themselves, or to improve their fortunes, by investing in durable or apparently durable assets which were rising most rapidly in price. The shenanigans of the stock exchanges, the fraudulent claims of the offshore promoters, the sudden passions for oil drilling, Scotch whisky stocks or first-growth clarets, all played supporting roles in a larger drama in which the main plot was the upward surge in public spending.

In six key countries of the West, governments raised spending by 51% in four years—much of it wasted, some of it well spent, but all in response to preconceived or supposed demands from the citizens for goods and services which allegedly only the public sector could provide. Nor was it only central governments that swelled the public sector's appetite. Local governments chipped in strongly on their own account. New York City is a microcosm of the catastrophe. Year after year the amount which the city's leaders wanted to spend exceeded the revenues which the taxpaying public was willing to provide. The gap was filled by borrowings, or by pretenses that the spending didn't exist, until the city, unable to raise its revenues by enough to cover the mounting interest payments on its accumulated debt, faced that monstrous 1975-76 deficit of $641 million.

Between 1956 and 1974 the numbers of state and local government employees in the United States rose from just over 5 million to around 11.5 million; at that point the bureaucratic army represented nearly 15% of total nonagricultural employment, compared to under a tenth eighteen years before. Most other governments, local and national, were only slightly more willing than New York's to raise enough revenue to cover their spending, or conversely, to cut their spending to fit their revenue. In the period 1968-72, spending in the OECD countries outran economic growth by eight percentage points. That may sound minute, but applied to the billions upon billions of national income, it produced shocking results: in 1972, when the OECD nations reported a combined rise in output of $351 billion, inflation accounted for $225 *billion* of the rise.

It was mainly through government overspending that the world money supply ($92.7 billion in 1970) virtually doubled by 1973. Almost all the increases took place in holdings of currency. By May 1975, the International Monetary Fund was reporting that the total was $228.7 billion, a rise of 147% in only five years. Even that grossly understated the true rate of inflation, since the large gold element in world reserves was valued at $42.20, when a realistic figure would have been well over double.

The rulers of the West showed themselves no wiser than the monarchs of sixteenth-century Spain, who destroyed their economies in a flood of gold and silver mined from the New World. There was a basic contrast, however. The Spanish monarchs didn't know what they were doing. Their OECD descendants, chasing too few goods with too much money no less recklessly, believed they knew what they did, and reckoned it was very respectable. As usual, they were listening to the teaching of an earlier generation—that of John Maynard Keynes. The great economist had proved that in recessions, the government, either by spending more or taxing less, or both, could fill the "deflationary gap." Thus budget deficits became virtues.

But the idea was that deficits would be used only at time of recession. After the war, governments eagerly boosted spending in relation to income in lean economic years, but wouldn't reverse engines in fat years. Anyway, they tended to embark on ambitious programs that committed billions of public revenues for years in advance.

The apotheosis of this maltreatment of Keynes

came with the work of President John F. Kennedy's economic advisers, led by Walter Heller. Heller designed a camouflage called "the full employment surplus." The theory, which in hindsight has far less logic than Sam Goldwyn's "include me out," was that, so long as the Federal budget *would* have been in surplus *if* the economy had been operating at full employment, it didn't matter how large a deficit the government ran at a time of less than full employment.

The argument was roughly the same as that of a bankrupt who affirms that, if only his income hadn't dropped, he wouldn't have gone broke. The Heller school was arguing that, so long as the total level of demand in the economy was below the potential level of supply, the government could spend almost as much money as it liked.

An enormous number of questions were begged: what, for instance, is full employment? Are there no limits to the amount which the citizens can owe themselves as both beneficiaries and holders of the national debt? But the main begged question was this: if the government couldn't expand its spending in relation to its revenues without enlarging the money supply (and it evidently couldn't), and if the supply of goods and services in the economy was either declining or not expanding fast enough (and by definition that was happening), then how could inflation be avoided? It couldn't, but the problem was ignored because the monetary economists, and monetary theory, were then almost as unfashionable as the flat-earthers.

One reason for that, in turn, was that permanent restraint on the growth of the money supply, as advocated by a voice crying in the wilderness, Chicago's Professor Milton Friedman, would have placed permanent restraint on the growth of public spending. Governments only have three sources of funds worth mentioning: taxes, borrowing and inflation. Friedmanite policies would certainly have restricted the amount of borrowing and would probably have kept inflation at very low levels.

Inflation is only a variation on the first two sources of public funds. The State, when it issues loans, borrows the taxpayer's money in bank notes of one denomination and repays the debt in dollar bills of much lower value, so turning a profit on the deal—at the taxpayers' expense. At the same time, under a so-called progressive tax system, the State reaps a hefty (unearned) reward simply because taxpayers who are earning exactly the same amount in terms of purchasing power are pushed into higher tax brackets, forcing them to hand over a larger percentage of an identical real income.

So without having to lift a finger, raise a tax or pass a law, the politicians, under inflation, can lay their hands on more and more of the people's wealth. In fairness, few, if any, politicians realized that this was the name of their game. The process of robbing the taxpayer of his money by failing to adjust for inflation is referred to by euphemisms like "the buoyancy of the revenue" or "fiscal drag."

In reality, public finance doesn't gain much benefit from these windfall gains: inflation pushes up government's costs like anybody else's, which means that the budget deficit tends to rise rather than fall, which means still more borrowing, which means still more expansion of the money supply, which means still more inflation. So the vicious circle is perpetuated.

The damage, moreover, isn't confined to people's incomes. Not only have the same inflationary forces reduced people's real wealth, but the capital taxes levied by all governments have similarly taken a bigger and bigger bite from smaller and smaller real sums. Progressive scales of inheritance tax, like progressive rates of income tax, snare progressively less wealthy fortunes, again without any benefit of legislation, or any opportunity for the fleeced to protest or defend themselves. Worse still: governments have been levying taxes on capital gains that have never materialized.

If you bought your stock in 1965 at 100 and saw it tripled by 1970, you might easily have suffered a halving of its value in 1975. If you sold out, in disgust and disappointment, or from sheer necessity, the difference would have been taxed as profit—even though 100 in 1965 might have needed to double by January 1975 merely to keep pace with the declining value of money.

The same fiscal rot that decomposed investors' capital in this way also affected investors on the income side. Corporate taxes are based on profits which became increasingly fictitious as time and inflation went on. In a year of 12% inflation, a company, even if it used the last in, first out method of stock evaluation, needed to raise profits by more than 12% to cover the rising cost of replacing its assets. If it recorded a 12% rise, the tax bill would only amount in step—because the corporation tax, at least, isn't progressive. But in reality the company might not have been making any surplus at all.

If it paid out a higher dividend, all the same, the recipients, since they were caught in a progressive tax system, paid the penalty. A 12% dividend hike was no real increase. But the tax on that truly static dividend might well be a higher proportion of the sum paid. These injustices, moreover, have been piled on top of a system of double taxation that for years, especially in the United States, has penalized savings placed in equities more than any other form.

The average U.S. company pays 35% of its profits in tax. Any money placed in its equity is more than likely to be post-tax money: that is, to get $100 to put in the stock, a man in the 35% tax bracket has had to earn nearly $154. His share of the earnings, say, is $20: $7 levied in tax leaves the poor chap with $13. If all of that is paid out in dividends, another $4.55 gets snatched.

Out of the $174 the Internal Revenue Service has collected $65.55, taxing the yield on the man's savings ($11.55 out of $20) at a far higher rate (57% against 35%) than his earnings. The system might have been designed to discourage the ancient economic virtues of saving and thrift, even in a noninflationary period. But with surging inflation, this combination of rising tax brackets and taxes on nonexistent profits deprived the investor of his real income and then set him up as a sitting duck for capital taxes on his nonexistent or overstated gains. With government also demanding more and more of the available savings to finance its deficits, the result was to raise serious doubts over industry's ability to finance itself.

As it is, U.S. business was forced by inadequate real profits to borrow $1.60 for each $1 of internal cash in 1974—against only 60 cents of borrowing per internal $1 a decade before. The tax monster not only drained blood from industry, but its claw marks and bites tore gaping social wounds which demanded desperate healing attempts. Deficit spending and overexpansion of the money supply pushed up basic prices beyond people's threshold of tolerance. So prices were held down by controls, and the holes in profits were filled by subsidies. But a subsidy is, of course, a tax. It means that revenue has to be diverted from somewhere else, and replaced either by a new tax or by borrowing (which is delayed tax) or by inflation (which is a concealed tax). Efforts to appease the monster only increase its appetite.

In the sixties, under the influence of John Kenneth Galbraith's *The Affluent Society*, Westerners largely swallowed the thesis of public squalor and private affluence. If public spending on schools fell behind the need, while that on washing machines soared, plainly the order of priorities had to be reversed. The argument led inexorably to the easy conclusion that public spending was essentially good, and that anxiety about its total was misplaced, because most public money went back into the private economy in wages or payments for goods and services, or in direct payments to the neediest members of society. Quite apart from the logical difficulties—the more the State bought, the less there would be for citizens to buy with the money the State returned to them—the idea ignored the tremendous leakage in the transfer system.

If the State uses resources only a degree more wastefully than the private sector, the whole economy is impoverished by increased transfers from the latter to the former. And there is plenty of evidence that the State is more profligate, as would be expected from any operation that faces no competition of any kind. Ignoring the giant boondoggles in aerospace, etc., the figures indicate that government is less careful about its spending and less likely to resist pressures to spend more. In 1955-73 Federal civilian employees in the United States pushed up their earnings by 5.9% a year. State and local government was a little further behind, with 5.6%. The figures compared to a 4.7% rise for all private industry, and cumulatively they meant that in the decade Federal employees had received pay rises worth half as much again as those of workers in the private sector.

The tax monster took in more and more money, misspent more and more of it and returned less to the saving classes than to the lower income groups. (Even so, the impact of regressive taxes, such as customs duties, tobacco imposts and sales levies, plus the abrupt transition in the tax system from nil income tax to taxpaying, meant that many poor people paid as much proportionately in tax as the rich.) But the more the monster forces the saving classes to spend or makes it difficult for its members to save, the more it eats away at the seed corn of future growth and future tax revenues.

In recession, government revenue is reduced, but the demand for public services is actually boosted—with emergency or standby measures to deal with unemployment and bankruptcies added to the unchanged requirements of education, defense, security and the rest. To take the New York City case as an example, the city tries to cover its huge spending out of revenue, but the high taxation combines with other factors to drive business and individuals out of the metropolitan area, reducing the revenue base and forcing the city either to borrow or to tax still more.

In much the same way, high spending at the level of the central State, unless it is forced by some automatic discipline to resist fiscal temptation, leads on to high taxation, which in turn weakens the revenue base. The fall in the profitability of large companies in the West in the sixties went on too long to be considered merely cyclical, and it led directly to the excess of debt and shortage of capital in private companies which marked the beginning of the seventies.

On the conventional measures of profit, which undoubtedly overstated true resources, the median profitability of *Fortune's* 500 largest American firms slid from 11.8% in 1965 to 9.1% in 1972. The rise in the next two years largely reflected the record inflation which undermined corporate finances still more insidiously. It wasn't so much the direct loss of real tax revenue that mattered in this context as the indirect effects on investment, economic growth and employment (although the direct effects in the United States, which gets 12% of its revenue from corporations as opposed to 5% in Germany and 8% in Britain, are not to be sneezed at).

With taxes rising as a proportion of national income, and with the impact of inflation on both taxability and resources of all kinds, comes an erosion of personal wealth. The erosion is subtle and gradual, perhaps not even noticed. People in America still regard $100,000 a year as the level of making it big, just as people in Britain would settle on £10,000. The target figures have not changed in years, even though their true value has halved in little more than a decade. Expectations and worth are equally devalued, while the government, the theoretical guardian of money, aids and abets its destruction.

The effect is exactly the same as if government bonds were issued with the condition that they would be repaid, at a time of stable money, as a discount from the original purchase price, and that the interest would bear successively higher tax charges. Nobody, of course, would buy such bonds except at pistol point. Yet that is what was offered—and purchased, because no better security seemed to exist.

The effect of the government's semirubber checks

was that of all bad money. As Gresham's law of 1558 states, bad money drives out good. The low reward for savings deposited in the traditional resting places of conservative money forced us to look elsewhere. If a real return of 3%, with the capital preserved in total safety, had been available on blue-chip stocks, how many of us would have been tempted by equities which offered lower yields and put the capital's safety in grave doubt?

The insecurity of government bonds, which was the product of government-induced inflation, gave the con men their opening. They could and did hawk their wares as safer than gilt-edged. Yet U.S. Treasury bills in the decade 1964-75—about as a stodgy an investment as could be imagined—actually outperformed Wall Street by a small but decisive margin. Legg Mason's Washington Service in August 1975 reported that $100 placed in the bills at the end of 1964 would have grown to $175.31 by May 1975—or a rotten $104.34 in uninflated dollars. But $100 invested in the stocks composing Standard & Poor's 500, even with dividends reinvested, would have got no further than $152.80—a loss of $9.05 in real terms. Only in four years out of ten did the cumulative gain on the 500 come out ahead of the Treasury bill.

To arrive at the same, or rather a worse end, investors had been forced to pass from peaks to valleys, from exaggerated joy to dreadful despair. In part, this was merely a reflection of the business cycle. But the economic and fiscal policies of government exaggerated the swings by undermining their monetary basis. The tax monster, in cutting its wide swath through the finances of the West, had raised a final paradox: the equity investment that had been so dramatically encouraged by the monster's inflationary excesses could now only be saved if somehow the monster could be persuaded to cease and desist

22 From Him That Hath, Too Much Is Required

In the year of calamity, 1974, it was fashionable, especially among the enemies of the economic order, to argue that capitalism was on its last legs. The quadrupling of oil prices by the best organized, most powerful and most open cartel in history was, however, clearly more the symptom than the cause of the crisis in capitalism. The two factors that generated the cartel's new power were the worldwide inflation (in which some other commodity prices actually rose faster than oil) and the Arab-Israeli conflict, which a left-wing theoretician could readily present as one of the last colonialist wars. The demolition of savings by inflation, the steep rise in unemployment, the instability of governments, the bank failures, the crash of the stock markets—they all supported the theory of a system on the edge of ruin.

The Second Great Crash had been predicted by the most acute historian of the First, John Kenneth Galbraith. The warning message in his book *The Great Crash*, to the effect that what had happened once could happen again, didn't seem based on any stronger predictive grounds than observation of human nature and the evidence that speculative excesses could surge into life as easily under the new order as the old. This economic Cassandra's wisdom appeared essentially no different from the repeated noises offstage of a pessimistic market seer like Eliot Janeway.

Prophets of gloom had a glorious time in the Second Great Crash, although their vindication merely reflected the uninspiring truth that, if you predict disaster often enough, you must one day be proved right. Galbraith, however, was in an intellectual class by himself, as he demonstrated in 1975 by saying correctly that his predicted Second Crash had not only come, but gone. The crisis of capitalism, so far as it was a crisis in the stock markets, was over.

By late 1975 it was also clear that the inflationary forces, far from becoming self-perpetuating, were in retreat before the defending forces: monetary restraint, slackening demand, and inflation itself. Like a virus creating antibodies, inflation is an engine of deflation. The rises in price choke off demand. As demand falls, surpluses of goods emerge. In the effort to dispose of the surplus, producers and distributors cut prices, voluntarily or under duress.

The process can be clearly seen in free, unrigged markets. Despite the oil cartel, oil prices came under formidable pressure as consumers cut back in the wake of the price rises. The pressure burst through in tanker rates, which were not protected by the cartel, and slumped so acutely that new supertankers went straight from the building yards into mothballs. Copper was another illustration, falling by two-thirds in a matter of months. Falls in the prices of New York cooperative apartments, London office blocks, fine wines and cut-price durables were all symptoms of the same automatic correction.

The Second Great Crash was a straightforward correction in the greatest market of them all: the ownership of industry in the West. What came down fell for much the same reason as the price of copper. Speculation had piled on the back of genuine increases in demand to drive prices up beyond the point of reality: in other words, past the level where people were prepared to buy more of the commodity. When demand disappears, any supply automatically becomes excessive, and the collapse of prices is inevitable.

That is the beauty of markets, and their ultimate justification. They allow basic economic forces to work, to restore balance where disequilibrium has appeared. In this sense, a stock market in which IBM sells on a multiple of 15 (in mid-1975) is far healthier than one (in mid-1970) where the relevant figure is 34, although the victim/investor may feel no happier about the treatment than an amputee at losing a limb.

The situation would be far from healthy, indeed downright sick, if the Second Great Crash had become self-feeding, like the first. No chain reaction developed—partly because the base of borrowed money was much smaller than in the 1929 boom-and-bust; partly because the financial institutions were not hopelessly dependent on equities; partly because the gaping rents which were torn in the financial structure were hastily sewn up by the financial authorities; partly because the automatic regulators of the Welfare State prevented the recessions around the West from gathering truly destructive pace.

The drop in the American gross national product came to only 10%, and for every American man or woman out of work, nine were gainfully employed. Moreover, the human sufferings of the recession, while real and painful, bore no comparison with the horrors of the Depression, mainly because of the cushions provided by the years of past affluence, and by the aforesaid tax-paid benefits of the Welfare State. Twelve months after the prophets of doom had reached their apogee, with the fainter-hearted citizens stocking up bombproof hideaways with food, weapons and gold coins, the crisis had lost its burning intensity—even though the problem of combining full employment with expansion and stable money now seemed to be beyond the scope of Keynesian or even neo-Keynesian economics.

The crisis, however, was the work of the disciples of Keynes, not in following the great man's teachings, but in abusing them. Reasonable stability of prices is a potent force for economic expansion; in a noninflationary situation, people happily invest more at lower prices (i.e., interest rates) and still become genuinely richer simply with the passage of time, because the marvels of compound interest are not overtaken by the evils of declining money values. Deficit financing, over-stimulation of the economy in the upward phases of the cycle, balance of payments transgressions—all these were insults to the memory and teaching of Keynes.

But if mistakes of economic management set the scene for the great showdown, profound changes in the business system were also responsible for the direction taken by events. The sweeping nature of the changes had not gone unnoticed, even if their significance was misunderstood. Trends such as the growing scale of the multinationals, the decline of the shareholder as the professional manager rose, the tendency toward amalgamations in many markets and across markets, the rising influence of the institutions on corporate ownership—these trends had been inescapably obvious for a long time.

The underlying shift is that from owner-management to manager-management. With rare exceptions, the multiplication of the multinationals has expressed managerial rather than proprietorial drive. The main result of the divorce between ownership and control has been to create a management machine with access to far more money than the Rothschild family mustered at its zenith, but whose objectives are necessarily fuzzy. The managers' personal ambitions—high present living standards and a comfortable future retirement—needn't relate to the progress of the corporation. Whether a company girdles the globe or confines itself to America is a matter of total choice: no categorical imperative drives the corporation abroad. The motives that led the Rothschilds to fan out over Europe were highly personal and highly profitable; they have no true reflection in the manager-managed company.

The special nature of the problem can be seen more clearly by contemplating the many remaining wholly owned companies. Where the proprietor is the sole shareholder, no philosophical difficulties arise. The owner is as free as any old Rothschild to develop the business as he chooses: if that means, for instance, inability to pay dividends for a couple of years, because of a heavy capital investment program, then only he, as shareholder, suffers loss of income. The motivation of the company is what he and he alone chooses to make it, simply because he personally represents two sections of the tripartite nature of the firm (owner, manager and employee). And unless he can persuade the employees to cooperate in his ambitions, those plans are highly unlikely to be realized, in this life or the next.

The survival of successful private firms into the era of progressive or repressive taxation and of big-company domination is not merely an interesting curiosity, a modern anachronism. The continued existence of groups like the Johnson's Wax family satrapy not only testifies to the power of uncomplicated motives, but also re-asserts a simple fact of business life. For a private firm to survive in acceptable splendor, the prime condition is high profitability. As they have no equity to mobilize, the proprietors cannot carelessly merge, or easily expand the capital base. That in turn limits their ability to run into debt. Because they cannot offer glossy substitutes like stock options, they are thrown back on employing corporate servants who respond well to good jobs and high salaries. None of this exempts the private company from the weaknesses of organizations large and small. But it imposes essential elements of discipline.

The diffusion of ownership in public companies is admirable in some respects, such as weakening the power of wealthy oligarchs and enabling prodigies of financing, in enterprises ranging from railroads to North Sea oil. But it has the disadvantages of forcing the masses to share in corporate failure. If the private company overspends, or underinvests, or disguises losses as profits, only the proprietor, his employees and the creditors suffer. But the shareholders in public companies not only have the sins of nonproprietorial managers visited on their heads; unlike creditors, they are helpless.

Society has recognized and accepted the equal helplessness of the depositor in a bank. The crimes of mismanagement that undermined an institution like the Franklin National were little different from the managerial misdemeanors of a Penn Central. Yet the resources of the Federal Government and the banking industry were hastily mobilized to ensure that nobody with money in the bank lost a dime. Those who had in effect placed their funds in the care of the railroad directors (many of whom happened to be bankers) were left to sink or swim, just like the unfortunates whose money was locked up in IOS mutual funds or the real-estate ramps. Investment in the ownership of industry, it seems, is a speculative affair, in which *caveat emptor* applies. The shareholder has all the risks of the proprietor, but in practical terms none of his power.

Sadly for the shareholders, the managers, who do possess nearly all the power of the proprietor, have decided to emulate him, or at least his fortune. A respectable theme song of big business is the necessity to make young managers think of their pieces of the corporation as "a business like their own." The attitude ignores the crucial difference between whole-hog proprietorship and the professional: the latter has a fiduciary responsibility to the shareholders which is, or should be, as paramount as the obligation of a bank to its depositors.

Yet no sanctions compel the manager to execute his duty; no defenses worth speaking of protect the shareholder against managers who neglect their fiduciary role. The little old lady in Dubuque, or, to take a less sentimental case, the physician in Great Neck, have the investment of their savings in industry treated with little respect. If the company goes bust, we shareholders are last in the queue to collect our money, after the bankers, the secured creditors, the loan stockholders, etc.

The justification of this maltreatment in the old days was that the equity holder, unlike the lender of fixed interest money, was entitled to a share of the profits. The risk of being wiped out was the price the equity holder paid for this privilege. But where is the privilege in modern times? For decades, dividend payouts have compared unfavorably with interest yields: undistributed, plowed-back profits, ostensibly belonging to the equity holders, often yield negligible or wholly inadequate returns.

The equity holder, in return for taking all of the risks, has received short rations in the way of reward, a deprivation faithfully reflected by the collapse in stock market values. Not surprisingly, distinguished accountants are beginning to challenge the whole concept of "free" (that is, cost-less) equity capital.

A company needs $50 million, say. If it raises the money by a new issue of shares, no charge is made against profits, and those who hand over the money have no security. If the same sum is raised via a loan stock, the interest (unlike the dividend on the shares) is charged against profits, and the borrowing is fully secured against some of the company's assets. Nor is it any use pointing out (correctly, in legal fact) that all the uncharged assets belong to the equity holders. Owners of last resort (as in W. T. Grant, as in Penn Central) only get their hands on the goods when all other claims have been met.

In justice, equity capital should receive at least the same return as the going rate available on alternative investments, and these dividends, like interest, should rank as a prior charge against income. If those dividends were tax deductible, as any interest paid, the profits reported by many corporations would wither away. Instead, the prevailing idiocy allows companies to report huge returns on shareholder's equity or "invested capital," when in reality only microscopic proportions of that return are made available to the shareholder.

For instance, ITT reported an 11.2% return on stockholders' equity in 1974. But the total payment on that capital ($4.1 billion) was $206 million, or 5%. With $3.6 billion of debt, the interest and other financial charges paid came to $368 million. Thus, although the shareholders take great risks, and the fixed interest lenders virtually none, the former receive the *lower*, not the higher yield.

If the alleged identity of interest among directors, managers and investors truly existed, such questions would at least be confronted by the corporations of the West. But directors and managers, who are, as we have seen, effectively the same people, have no interest in losing the supply of uncharged capital which the shareholders provide, like it or not.

Suppose that a company has $10 million available after tax and interest. If it pays out $5 million in dividends and retains the rest, that provides, at a time of 10% money, $500,000 in pretax profits without any directorial effort whatsoever. If all the $10 million were paid out to the shareholders, and the $5 million had to be replaced from another source at 10% plus, then there would be a $500,000-plus charge *against* profits. So the preference of the corporate establishment for plowing back is totally explicable.

In the above case, you might (if you hadn't been enlightened by these pages) prefer your company to be half a million up rather than down. But the half-million, of course, comes out of your own pocket; and there is no guarantee, because of the fragile link between the market and the company results, that you will receive any reward, here or in heaven, for putting the profits above your pocket.

What is true at the level of higher financial strategy applies as strongly at the lower level of managerial money. The shareholder-manager conflict emerges clearly if a grossly overgenerous stock option scheme is put up for approval. So most schemes are not gross, because boards of directors wish to avoid opposition from stockholders; most of us, again, fail to realize that profits from the most decent of option schemes must also come out of our own heavily raided pockets.

The profitable option, at the moment of issue, is worth more than the option holder paid, which is another way of saying that it is worth more than the shareholder is receiving at the time of selling part of his equity interest. This unequal deal is based on the convenient theory that managers and investors have an equal stake in seeing the share price rise.

On the upside, the theory works—although inadequately, since there is no good reason why the manager should benefit more, and with far less risk, than the investor, as he does under an option scheme. But on the downside the theory collapses: the manager under the most popular schemes simply loses potential profit, while the investor loses real capital. The option merely enshrines the conventional nonsense of the go-go years, which was to persuade managers (very easily) to pay attention to the short-term behavior of the stock market rather than the long-term interests of the investor.

For all the concrete abuse we suffered—from neglect, appropriation of our savings and castration of our powers—investors became steadily more unpopular as the sixties turned into the seventies. None of the critics could explain, nor did they even bother to ask, why a man, woman or institution putting unsecured funds into the equity of a company was in any way less worthy than the bank that extended the same firm a secured loan callable at short notice. Putting money into industry was respectable, in other words, so long as it involved only indirect ownership of the assets, as opposed to a direct property right in some of those assets.

On Wall Street, the ratio of dividends to earnings of the Dow stocks fell from over 70% in 1961 to 38% —its lowest level ever—in 1974. In other words, where 70 cents of the profit dollar had gone to stockholders, only 38 cents reached them thirteen years later. Yet it was thought right and proper for dividend payments to be frozen at a time when interest payments on loans by the same companies were being allowed to achieve the highest levels on postwar record. Plainly, ownership is the essence of the attacker's position. The odium once directed at a Henry Ford, who personally reigned over the life and work of hundreds of thousands of men and women, has been transferred to innocents whose only sin is to purchase the titles to ownership.

The ownership is a fiction, in the sense that the naked investor's ability to influence the managers is infinitesimal; in any event, we seldom choose or wish to try to influence them. To be maltreated by the State for wielding a fictitious power adds insult to injury; it is not compatible with the capitalist system as it is supposed to exist. If companies are to be managed for the benefit of the managers, and if the investor is to be pushed further down the queue by the modern upsurge of worker representation, then capitalism on the postwar model is genuinely dead, although in a sense different from that used by the mongers of doom.

Unfortunately, nothing in sight can replace the corpse—except the disciplines that would be imposed by an authentic shareholding democracy. A system like that, imposing high fiduciary and performance standards on the managerial elite, would remove forever some of the febrile excesses that made the Second Great Crash, for much less economic cause, as traumatic in its impact on savings as the First.

Some of the remedies are obvious: tax reforms that will treat dividend payments on equal terms with interest and end the present discouragement of payouts; accountancy reforms that will bar the deceitful game of maximizing reported earnings; legal reforms that will redress the balance of power between manager and investor by removing the defects, such as stock options and the cosy dependence of auditors on management, that currently distort the relationship: regulatory reforms that will make the seller, not the buyer, beware. While obvious, the needed reforms are politically and sometimes technically rough. Nor will they be adopted or effective so long as the fate of investors (even though today, with the growth of institutional savings, that means nearly everybody) is treated as immaterial.

As it is, you the shareholder, harmless and all but helpless, have been through your biggest battering for forty years. Yet you are still supposed to supply the underpinning for most of the economic system of the West. In the corporate liquidity crisis that accompanied the Crash, the last remaining large private groups suddenly seem to be oases of stability in a turbulent world. Their investors at least didn't see fortunes blown up like hot-air balloons, only to burst into flames.

From Him That Hath, Too Much Is Required

The brightest ray of light is the possibility that you will remember your burns, so that another inflation of stock prices, with the inevitable subsequent deflation, will not happen again for that reason alone. But if the lessons have not been learned, and you try once more to reach Utopian financial salvation through the stock market, the Second Great Crash will not be merely a recrudescence of the First. It will prove to be a trailer for the Third; and the Third might be Last.

23 If You Keep Your Money Under the Mattress, Don't Smoke in Bed

Some of the protection that naked investors need will have to be provided by others—people who haven't been any great shakes at the job in the recent past. But do you remember our friendly Italian economist, Pareto, and his 80-20 rule? It applies to you: 20% of the circumstances are not under your control, but the remaining four-fifths are. Your job is to control what you can.

That means listening closely to what you are told —especially by yourself. You have to decide what you want from investing, what you're prepared to settle for, whether you want a bumpy ride or an easy cruise, what safety belts you're prepared to fasten, what methods you will adopt. As these pages have shown, you're wiser than you may have thought—and anybody who offers you universal solutions or infallible get-rich-quick methods is a great deal more foolish than he may appear.

The equipment you need, in addition to an inquiring and skeptical mind, is very simple. A pocket calculator, a ruled ledger, a ball-point pen and a daily newspaper will look after your basic needs. Further information can always be obtained from your broker —that's what he is there for. If he doesn't give you the help you need, find somebody who will. If you subscribe to an investment service, adopt the same approach: you want information on which you can form your own judgments, not tips that are substitutes for your own decisions.

Don't put yourself behind the eight ball by trying to maximize your money. How big is maximum? You want to hit identified and feasible targets. If your investing carries you over and above the target line, all well and good. But your overriding objective is a minimum, not a maximum—the minimum level at which you feel that you and your money are being reasonably well looked after.

Of course, you may be in the game for the fun. Very few poker players win all the time, or even most of the time. If you want to play at investment, using your stock certificates as chips, that's fine, too. But you will have more fun if you follow our rules and try to outwit and outdo the professionals in the world's biggest game of five-card stud.

You have an advantage over them. By and large, the pros move in packs. You are a free-lance and can move against or away from the pack without fear of exposing yourself before your colleagues. And that, truly, is the overall lesson which the naked investor has to learn. The disasters that we have all passed through were created by the conventional wisdom. The rich rewards go to those who are unconventionally wise. If the conventional ones tell you that you're being foolish—well, maybe the truth is that you are a very well-dressed investor indeed.

It could be that, having come along with us through

all the minefields of the stock market, you don't like the idea of setting out again through the same terrain. But no other reasonably liquid investment in the whole wide world offers the same potential, if you manage your own behavior logically and consistently, as the array of common stocks. There is risk, of course: but the risk/reward ratio is in favor of the prepared mind.

You can still stay out. That's your privilege. But if you're going to keep your money under the mattress, don't smoke in bed.